Practice the Nelson Denny!

Practice Test Questions for the
Nelson Denny Test

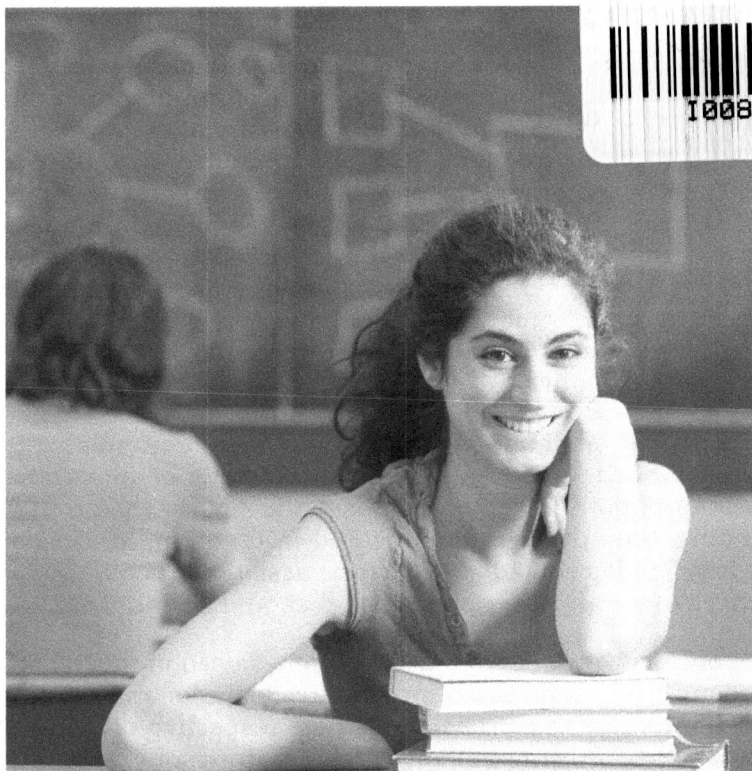

Published by
Blue Butterfly Books™

Copyright Notice

Published by
Blue Butterfly Books
Victoria BC Canada
Printed in the USA

Team Members for this publication

Editor: Sheila Hynes H.BA M.E.S.
Contributor: Dr. C. Gregory
Contributor: Dr. G. A. Stocker DDS
Contributor: D. A. Stocker M. Ed.
Contributor: Brian Stocker MA

ISBN-13: 978-0993753794 (Blue Butterfly Books)

ISBN-10: 0993753795

Sustainability and Eco-Responsibility

Here at *Blue Butterfly Books*^{TM}, trees are valuable to Mother Earth and the health and wellbeing of everyone. Minimizing our ecological footprint and effect on the environment, we choose Create Space, an eco-responsible printing company.

Electronic routing of our books reduces greenhouse gas emissions, worldwide. When a book order is received, the order is filled at the printing location closest to the client. Using environmentally friendly publishing technology, of the Espresso book printing machine, *Blue Butterfly Books*^{TM} are printed as they are requested, saving thousands of books, and trees over time. This process offers the stable and viable alternative keeping healthy sustainability of our environment.

All paper is acid-free, and interior paper stock is made from 30% post-consumer waste recycled material. Safe for children, Create Space also verifies the materials used in the print process are all CPSIA-compliant.

By purchasing this *Blue Butterfly Books*^{TM}, you have supported Full Recovery and Preservation of The Karner Blue Butterfly . Our logo is the Karner Blue Butterfly, Lycaeides melissa samuelis, a rare and beautiful butterfly species whose only flower for propogation is the blue lupin flower. The Karner Butterfly is mostly found in the Great Lakes Region of the U.S.A. Recovery planning is in action, for the return of Karner Blue in Canada led by the National Recovery Strategy. The recovery goals and objectives are aimed at recreating suitable habitats for the butterfly and encourage the growth of blue lupines - the butterfly's natural ideal habitat.

For more info on the Karner Blue Butterfly , feel free to visit:

http://www.albanypinebush.org/conservation/wildlife-management/karner-blue-butterfly-recovery

http://www.wiltonpreserve.org/conservation/karner-blue-butterfly.

http://www.natureconservancy.ca/en/what-we-do/resource-centre/featured-species/karner_blue.html.

Contents

Getting Started with the Nelson Denny

CONGRATULATIONS! By deciding to take the Nelson Denny Reading Test, (NDRT) you have taken the first step toward a great future! Of course, there is no point in taking this important examination unless you intend to do your very best in order to earn the highest grade you possibly can. That means getting yourself organized and discovering the best approaches, methods and strategies to master the material. Yes, that will require real effort and dedication on your part but if you are willing to focus your energy and devote the study time necessary, before you know it you will be opening that letter of acceptance to the school of your dreams.

We know that taking on a new endeavour can be a little scary, and it is easy to feel unsure of where to begin. That's where we come in. This study guide is designed to help you improve your test-taking skills, show you a few tricks and increase both your competency and confidence.

The Nelson Denny Exam.

The Nelson Denny is composed of two subject areas, reading comprehension and vocabulary. Since how well you score in each of these areas will determine whether or not you get into the best school possible, it is important to be prepared. In the area of reading comprehension, examinees will be tested on their ability to comprehend reading passages, make inferences regarding those passages and draw logical conclusions. In the vocabulary section you will be tested on your word knowledge.

HOW THIS STUDY GUIDE IS ORGANIZED.

This study guide is divided into five sections. The first section, Getting Started, gives basic information about the Nelson Denny and how to make a study plan and schedule.

Chapter two, Self-Assessments will help you recognize your areas of strength and weakness. This will be a boon when it comes to managing your study time most efficiently; there is not much point of focusing on material you already have firmly under control. Instead, taking the self-assessments will show you where that time could be much better spent. The Self-Assessments have a few questions to quickly evaluate your understanding of material similar to what you will find on the Nelson Denny. If you do poorly in certain areas, simply work carefully through those sections in the tutorials and then try the self-assessment again. Chapter three contains two sets of practice test questions with questions similar in type and difficulty to the Nelson Denny.

Chapter four is an in-depth Tutorial on how to improve your vocabulary. If you are reading this book and studying for the Nelson Denny, you probably don't have time to use the most effective way to increase your vocabulary, which is reading all the time. Therefore, things being what they are, we offer fast and effective strategies for increasing your vocabulary, as well as two hundred practice questions.

While we seek to make our guide as comprehensive as possible, note that like all exams, the Nelson Denny Exam might be adjusted at some future point. New material might be added, or content that is no longer relevant or applicable might be removed. It is always a good idea to give the materials you receive when you register to take the Nelson Denny a careful review.

The Nelson Denny Exam Study Plan.

Now that you have made the decision to take the Nelson Denny, it is time to get started. Before you do another thing, you will need to figure out a plan of attack. The very best study tip is to start early! The longer you devote to regular study practice, the more likely you will be to retain the material and be able to access it quickly, and under stressful situations - like in an exam room! If you thought that 1 X 20 is the same as 2 X 10, guess what? It really is not, when it comes to study time. Reviewing material for just an hour per day over the course of 20 days is far better than studying for two hours a day for only 10 days. The more often you revisit a particular piece of information, the better you will know it. Not only will your grasp and understanding be better, but your ability to reach into your brain and quickly and efficiently pull out the tidbit you need, will be greatly enhanced as well.

The great Chinese scholar and philosopher Confucius believed that true knowledge could be defined as knowing both what you know and what you do not know. The first step in preparing for the Nelson Denny Exam is to assess your strengths and weaknesses. You may already have an idea of what you know and what you do not know, but evaluating yourself using our Self- Assessment modules for both Vocabulary and Reading Comprehension, will clarify the details.

MAKING A STUDY SCHEDULE.

To make your study time most productive you will need to develop a study plan. The purpose of the plan is to organize all the bits of pieces of information in such a way that you will not feel overwhelmed. Rome was not built in a day, and learning everything you will need to know to pass the Nelson Denny is going to take time, too. Arranging the material you need to learn into manageable chunks is the best way to go. Each study session should take you one step closer to your final goal and make you feel as though you have succeeded in accomplishing something. Your goal is simply to learn what you planned to learn during that particular session. Try to organize the content in such a way that each study session builds on previous ones. That way, you will retain the information, be better able to access it, and review the previous bits and pieces at the same time.

It makes sense to focus your study time on those subjects that need the most work but unless you create a visual chart for yourself, chances are good you will get confused in no time. First, write out what you need to study and how much time you want to devote to it. This is easy since the Nelson Denny is a pretty simple format, with only reading comprehension and vocabulary questions. Next, consider how many days you have before the test. Plan to take time off from studying on the day before the exam is scheduled. On the last day before the test, you will not learn anything and will probably only confuse yourself. Besides, giving yourself a little break means you will feel fresher on the day of the test.

Make a table with columns for the number of days before the test and rows for the number of hours you have available to study each day. We suggest working with half hour and one hour time slots; less than that means you will get set up to study and it will be time to quit, and more than an hour might result in mental fatigue.

Now you are ready to begin filling in the blanks. Give the most time to those subjects you need to study the most. It is also a good idea to assign your weakest subjects the most regular time slots. In fact, even just thirty minutes a day will help lock in the information you need. Of course, those subjects that you know like the back of your hand can be assigned the shortest blocks of time.

TIPS FOR MAKING A STUDY SCHEDULE.

Once you set a schedule that works, stick with it! Establish study sessions that are realistic. Blocking out study time that is too long or too short means you will be tempted to cheat. Instead, schedule study sessions that are reasonable and you will set yourself up for success!

Schedule breaks. Breaks are just as important as study time. Work out a rotation of studying and brief breaks that works for you.

Build up study time. If you find it hard to sit still and study for an hour at first, build up to it. Start with 20 minutes, and then take a break. Once you get used to 20-minute study sessions, increase the time to 30 minutes. Gradually work your way up to a full hour.

Forty minutes to an hour is optimal. Studying for longer is not productive. Studying for periods that are too short won't give you enough time to really learn anything.

Nelson Denny Practice Test Questions

Practice Test Questions Set I

THE PRACTICE TEST QUESTIONS PORTION PRESENTS QUESTIONS REPRE-SENTATIVE OF WHAT YOU CAN EXPECT TO FIND ON THE NELSON DENNY. However, they are not intended to match exactly what is on the NDRT.

For the best results, take the practice test questions as if it were the real exam. Set aside time when you will not be disturbed, and a location that is quiet and free of distractions. Read the instructions carefully, read each question carefully, and answer to the best of your ability.

Use the bubble answer sheets provided. When you have completed the practice questions, check your answer against the Answer Key and read the explanation provided.

Reading Comprehension Answer Sheet.

1. Ⓐ Ⓑ Ⓒ Ⓓ	11. Ⓐ Ⓑ Ⓒ Ⓓ	21. Ⓐ Ⓑ Ⓒ Ⓓ
2. Ⓐ Ⓑ Ⓒ Ⓓ	12. Ⓐ Ⓑ Ⓒ Ⓓ	22. Ⓐ Ⓑ Ⓒ Ⓓ
3. Ⓐ Ⓑ Ⓒ Ⓓ	13. Ⓐ Ⓑ Ⓒ Ⓓ	23. Ⓐ Ⓑ Ⓒ Ⓓ
4. Ⓐ Ⓑ Ⓒ Ⓓ	14. Ⓐ Ⓑ Ⓒ Ⓓ	24. Ⓐ Ⓑ Ⓒ Ⓓ
5. Ⓐ Ⓑ Ⓒ Ⓓ	15. Ⓐ Ⓑ Ⓒ Ⓓ	25. Ⓐ Ⓑ Ⓒ Ⓓ
6. Ⓐ Ⓑ Ⓒ Ⓓ	16. Ⓐ Ⓑ Ⓒ Ⓓ	26. Ⓐ Ⓑ Ⓒ Ⓓ
7. Ⓐ Ⓑ Ⓒ Ⓓ	17. Ⓐ Ⓑ Ⓒ Ⓓ	27. Ⓐ Ⓑ Ⓒ Ⓓ
8. Ⓐ Ⓑ Ⓒ Ⓓ	18. Ⓐ Ⓑ Ⓒ Ⓓ	28. Ⓐ Ⓑ Ⓒ Ⓓ
9. Ⓐ Ⓑ Ⓒ Ⓓ	19. Ⓐ Ⓑ Ⓒ Ⓓ	29. Ⓐ Ⓑ Ⓒ Ⓓ
10. Ⓐ Ⓑ Ⓒ Ⓓ	20. Ⓐ Ⓑ Ⓒ Ⓓ	30. Ⓐ Ⓑ Ⓒ Ⓓ

Nelson Denny Practice!

Vocabulary Answer Sheet

1. (A) (B) (C) (D)	21. (A) (B) (C) (D)	41. (A) (B) (C) (D)	61. (A) (B) (C) (D)
2. (A) (B) (C) (D)	22. (A) (B) (C) (D)	42. (A) (B) (C) (D)	62. (A) (B) (C) (D)
3. (A) (B) (C) (D)	23. (A) (B) (C) (D)	43. (A) (B) (C) (D)	63. (A) (B) (C) (D)
4. (A) (B) (C) (D)	24. (A) (B) (C) (D)	44. (A) (B) (C) (D)	64. (A) (B) (C) (D)
5. (A) (B) (C) (D)	25. (A) (B) (C) (D)	45. (A) (B) (C) (D)	65. (A) (B) (C) (D)
6. (A) (B) (C) (D)	26. (A) (B) (C) (D)	46. (A) (B) (C) (D)	66. (A) (B) (C) (D)
7. (A) (B) (C) (D)	27. (A) (B) (C) (D)	47. (A) (B) (C) (D)	67. (A) (B) (C) (D)
8. (A) (B) (C) (D)	28. (A) (B) (C) (D)	48. (A) (B) (C) (D)	68. (A) (B) (C) (D)
9. (A) (B) (C) (D)	29. (A) (B) (C) (D)	49. (A) (B) (C) (D)	69. (A) (B) (C) (D)
10. (A) (B) (C) (D)	30. (A) (B) (C) (D)	50. (A) (B) (C) (D)	70. (A) (B) (C) (D)
11. (A) (B) (C) (D)	31. (A) (B) (C) (D)	51. (A) (B) (C) (D)	71. (A) (B) (C) (D)
12. (A) (B) (C) (D)	32. (A) (B) (C) (D)	52. (A) (B) (C) (D)	72. (A) (B) (C) (D)
13. (A) (B) (C) (D)	33. (A) (B) (C) (D)	53. (A) (B) (C) (D)	73. (A) (B) (C) (D)
14. (A) (B) (C) (D)	34. (A) (B) (C) (D)	54. (A) (B) (C) (D)	74. (A) (B) (C) (D)
15. (A) (B) (C) (D)	35. (A) (B) (C) (D)	55. (A) (B) (C) (D)	75. (A) (B) (C) (D)
16. (A) (B) (C) (D)	36. (A) (B) (C) (D)	56. (A) (B) (C) (D)	76. (A) (B) (C) (D)
17. (A) (B) (C) (D)	37. (A) (B) (C) (D)	57. (A) (B) (C) (D)	77. (A) (B) (C) (D)
18. (A) (B) (C) (D)	38. (A) (B) (C) (D)	58. (A) (B) (C) (D)	78. (A) (B) (C) (D)
19. (A) (B) (C) (D)	39. (A) (B) (C) (D)	59. (A) (B) (C) (D)	79. (A) (B) (C) (D)
20. (A) (B) (C) (D)	40. (A) (B) (C) (D)	60. (A) (B) (C) (D)	80. (A) (B) (C) (D)

Questions 1 – 4 refer to the following passage.

Passage 1 - Infectious Disease

An infectious disease is a clinically evident illness resulting from the presence of pathogenic agents, such as viruses, bacteria, fungi, protozoa, multicellular parasites, and unusual proteins known as prions. Infectious pathologies are also called communicable diseases or transmissible diseases, due to their potential of transmission from one person or species to another by a replicating agent (as opposed to a toxin).

Transmission of an infectious disease can occur in many different ways. Physical contact, liquids, food, body fluids, contaminated objects, and airborne inhalation can all transmit infecting agents.

Transmissible diseases that occur through contact with an ill person, or objects touched by them, are especially infective, and are sometimes called contagious diseases. Communicable diseases that require a more specialized route of infection, such as through blood or needle transmission, or sexual transmission, are usually not regarded as contagious.

The term infectivity describes the ability of an organism to enter, survive and multiply in the host, while the infectiousness of a disease indicates the comparative ease with which the disease is transmitted. An infection however, is not synonymous with an infectious disease, as an infection may not cause important clinical symptoms. [2]

1. What can we infer from the first paragraph in this passage?

    a. Sickness from a toxin can be easily transmitted from one person to another.

    b. Sickness from an infectious disease can be easily transmitted from one person to another.

    c. Few sicknesses are transmitted from one person to another.

    d. Infectious diseases are easily treated.

2. What are two other names for infections' pathologies?

    a. Communicable diseases or transmissible diseases

    b. Communicable diseases or terminal diseases

    c. Transmissible diseases or preventable diseases

    d. Communicative diseases or unstable diseases

3. What does infectivity describe?

    a. The inability of an organism to multiply in the host.

    b. The inability of an organism to reproduce.

    c. The ability of an organism to enter, survive and multiply in the host.

    d. The ability of an organism to reproduce in the host.

4. How do we know an infection is not synonymous with an infectious disease?

    a. Because an infectious disease destroys infections with enough time.

    b. Because an infection may not cause important clinical symptoms or impair host function.

    c. We do not. The two are synonymous.

    d. Because an infection is too fatal to be an infectious disease.

Questions 5 – 8 refer to the following passage.

Low Blood Sugar

As the name suggest, low blood sugar is low sugar levels in the bloodstream. This can occur when you have not eaten properly and undertake strenuous activity, or when you are very hungry. When Low blood sugar occurs regularly and is ongoing, it is a medical condition called hypoglycemia. This condition can occur in diabetics and also in healthy adults.

Causes of low blood sugar can include excessive alcohol consumption, metabolic problems, stomach surgery, pancreas, liver or kidneys problems, as well as a side-effect of some medications.

Symptoms

There are different symptoms depending on the severity of the case.

Mild hypoglycemia can lead to feelings of nausea and hunger. The patient may also feel nervous, jittery and have fast heart beats. Sweaty skin, clammy and cold skin are likely symptoms.

Moderate hypoglycemia can result in short temperedness, confusion, nervousness, fear and blurring of vision. The patient may feel weak and unsteady.

Severe cases of hypoglycemia can lead to seizures, coma, fainting spells, nightmares, headaches, excessive sweats and severe tiredness.

Diagnosis of low blood sugar

A doctor can diagnosis this medical condition by asking the patient questions and testing blood and urine samples. Home testing kits are available for patients to monitor blood sugar levels. It is important to see a qualified doctor though. The doctor can administer tests to ensure that will safely rule out other medical conditions that could affect blood sugar levels.

Treatment

Quick treatments include drinking or eating foods and drinks with high sugar contents. Good examples include soda, fruit juice, hard candy and raisins. Glucose energy tablets can also help. Doctors may also recommend medications and well as changes in diet and exercise routine to treat chronic low blood sugar.

5. Based on the article, which of the following is true?

     a. a. Low blood sugar can happen to anyone.

     b. b. Low blood sugar only happens to diabetics.

     c. c. Low blood sugar can occur even.

     d. d. None of the statements are true.

6. Which of the following are the author's opinion?

     a. Quick treatments include drinking or eating foods and drinks with high sugar contents.

     b. None of the statements are opinions.

     c. This condition can occur in diabetics and also in healthy adults.

     d. There are different symptoms depending on the severity of the case

7. What is the author's purpose?

     a. To inform

     b. To persuade

     c. To entertain

     d. To analyze

8. Which of the following is not a detail?

     a. A doctor can diagnosis this medical condition by asking the patient questions and testing.

     b. A doctor will test blood and urine samples.

     c. Glucose energy tablets can also help.

     d. Home test kits monitor blood sugar levels.

Questions 9 – 11 refer to the following passage.

Passage 3 – Thunderstorms

The first stage of a thunderstorm is the cumulus stage, or developing stage. In this stage, masses of moisture are lifted upwards into the atmosphere. The trigger for this lift can be insulation heating the ground producing thermals, areas where two winds converge, forcing air upwards, or where winds blow over terrain of increasing elevation. Moisture in the air rapidly cools into liquid drops of water, which appears as cumulus clouds.

As the water vapor condenses into liquid, latent heat is released which warms the air, causing it to become less dense than the surrounding dry air. The warm air rises in an updraft through the process of convection (hence the term convective precipitation). This creates a low-pressure zone beneath the forming thunderstorm. In a typical thunderstorm, approximately 5×10^8 kg of water vapor is lifted, and the amount of energy released when this condenses is about equal to the energy used by a city of 100,000 in a month. [4]

9. The cumulus stage of a thunderstorm is the

    a. The last stage of the storm.

    b. The middle stage of the storm formation.

    c. The beginning of the thunderstorm.

    d. The period after the thunderstorm has ended.

10. One of the ways the air is warmed is

    a. Air moving downwards, which creates a high-pressure zone.

    b. Air cooling and becoming less dense, causing it to rise.

    c. Moisture moving downward toward the earth.

    d. Heat created by water vapor condensing into liquid.

11. Identify the correct sequence of events

a. Warm air rises, water droplets condense, creating more heat, and the air rises farther.

b. Warm air rises and cools, water droplets condense, causing low pressure.

c. Warm air rises and collects water vapor, the water vapor condenses as the air rises, which creates heat, and causes the air to rise farther.

d. None of the above.

Questions 12 – 14 refer to the following passage.

Passage 4 If You Have Allergies, You're Not Alone

People who experience allergies might joke that their immune systems have let them down or are seriously lacking. Truthfully though, people who experience allergic reactions or allergy symptoms during certain times of the year have heightened immune systems that are, "better" than those of people who have perfectly healthy but less militant immune systems.

Still, when a person has an allergic reaction, they are having an adverse reaction to a substance that is considered normal to most people. Mild allergic reactions usually have symptoms like itching, runny nose, red eyes, or bumps or discoloration of the skin. More serious allergic reactions, such as those to animal and insect poisons or certain foods, may result in the closing of the throat, swelling of the eyes, low blood pressure, an inability to breath, and can even be fatal.

Different treatments help different allergies, and which one a person uses depends on the nature and severity of the allergy. It is recommended to patients with severe allergies to take extra precautions, such as carrying an EpiPen, which treats anaphylactic shock and may prevent death, always in order for the remedy to be readily available and more effective. When an allergy is not so severe, treatments may be used just relieve a person of uncomfortable symptoms. Over the counter allergy medicines treat milder symptoms, and can be bought at any grocery store and used in moderation to help people with allergies live normally.

There are many tests available to assess whether a person has allergies or what they may be allergic to, and advances in these tests and the medicine used to treat patients continues to improve. Despite this fact, allergies still affect many people throughout the year or even every day. Medicines used to treat allergies have side effects of their own, and it is difficult to bring the body into balance with the use of medicine. Regardless, many of those who live with allergies are grateful for what is available and find it useful in maintaining their lifestyles.

12. According to this passage, it can be understood that the word "militant" belongs in a group with the words:

    a. sickly, ailing, faint

    b. strength, power, vigor

    c. active, fighting, warring

    d. worn, tired, breaking down

13. The author says that "medicines used to treat allergies have side effects of their own" to

    a. point out that doctors aren't very good at diagnosing and treating allergies

    b. argue that because of the large number of people with allergies, a cure will never be found

    c. explain that allergy medicines aren't cures and some compromise must be made

    d. argue that more wholesome remedies should be researched and medicines banned

14. It can be inferred that _____ recommend that some people with allergies carry medicine with them.

    a. the author

    b. doctors

    c. the makers of EpiPen

    d. people with allergies

Questions 15 – 18 refer to the following passage.

Passage 5 – Clouds

A cloud is a visible mass of droplets or frozen crystals floating in the atmosphere above the surface of the Earth or other planetary bodies. Another type of cloud is a mass of material in space, attracted by gravity, called interstellar clouds and nebulae. The branch of meteorology which studies clouds is called nephrology. When we are speaking of Earth clouds, water vapor is usually the condensing substance, which forms small droplets or ice crystal. These crystals are typically 0.01 mm in diameter. Dense, deep clouds reflect most light, so they appear white, at least from the top. Cloud droplets scatter light very efficiently, so the farther into a cloud light travels, the weaker it gets. This accounts for the gray or dark appearance at the base of large clouds. Thin clouds may appear to have acquired the color of their environment or background. [5]

15. What are clouds made of?

    a. Water droplets

    b. Ice crystals

    c. Ice crystals and water droplets

    d. Clouds on Earth are made of ice crystals and water droplets

16. The main idea of this passage is

a. Condensation occurs in clouds, having an intense effect on the weather on the surface of the earth.

b. Atmospheric gases are responsible for the gray color of clouds just before a severe storm happens.

c. A cloud is a visible mass of droplets or frozen crystals floating in the atmosphere above the surface of the Earth or other planetary body.

d. Clouds reflect light in varying amounts and degrees, depending on the size and concentration of the water droplets.

17. The branch of meteorology that studies clouds is called

a. Convection

b. Thermal meteorology

c. Nephology

d. Nephelometry

18. Why are clouds white on top and grey on the bottom?

a. Because water droplets inside the cloud do not reflect light, it appears white, and the farther into the cloud the light travels, the less light is reflected making the bottom appear dark.

b. Because water droplets outside the cloud reflect light, it appears dark, and the farther into the cloud the light travels, the more light is reflected making the bottom appear white.

c. Because water droplets inside the cloud reflects light, making it appear white, and the farther into the cloud the light travels, the more light is reflected making the bottom appear dark.

d. None of the above.

Questions 19 - 22 refer to the following recipe.

"When a Poet Longs to Mourn, He Writes an Elegy"

Poems are an expressive, especially emotional, form of writing. They have been present in literature virtually from the time civilizations invented the written word. Poets often portrayed as moody, secluded, and even troubled, but this is because poets are introspective and feel deeply about the current events and cultural norms they are surrounded with. Poets often produce the most telling literature, giving insight into the society and mind set they come from. This can be done in many forms.

The oldest types of poems often include many stanzas, may or may not rhyme, and are more about telling a story than experimenting with language or words. The most common types of ancient poetry are epics, which are usually extremely long stories that follow a hero through his journey, or ellegies, which are often solemn in tone and used to mourn or lament something or someone. The Mesopotamians are often said to have invented the written word, and their literature is among the oldest in the world, including the epic poem titled "Epic of Gilgamesh." Similar in style and length to "Gilgamesh" is "Beowulf," an ellegy poem written in Old English and set in Scandinavia. These poems are often used by professors as the earliest examples of literature.

The importance of poetry was revived in the Renaissance. At this time, Europeans discovered the style and beauty of ancient Greek arts, and poetry was among those. Shakespeare is the most well-known poet of the time, and he used poetry not only to write poems but also to write plays for the theater. The most popular forms of poetry during the Renaissance included villanelles, sonnets, as well as the epic. Poets during this time focused on style and form, and developed very specific rules and outlines for how an exceptional poem should be written.

As often happens in the arts, modern poets have rejected the constricting rules of Renaissance poets, and free form poems are much more popular. Some modern poems would read just like stories if they weren't arranged into lines and stanzas. It is difficult to tell which poems and poets will be the most important, because works of art often become more famous in hindsight, after the poet has died and society can look at itself without being in the moment. Modern poetry continues to develop, and will no doubt continue to change as values, thought, and writing continue to change.

Poems can be among the most enlightening and uplifting texts for a person to read if they are looking to connect with the past, connect with other people, or try to gain an understanding of what is happening in their time.

19. In summary, the author has written this passage

a. as a foreword that will introduce a poem in a book or magazine

b. because she loves poetry and wants more people to like it

c. to give a brief history of poems

d. to convince students to write poems

20. The author organizes the paragraphs mainly by

a. moving chronologically, explaining which types of poetry were common in that time

b. talking about new types of poems each paragraph and explaining them a little

c. focusing on one poet or group of people and the poems they wrote

d. explaining older types of poetry so she can talk about modern poetry

21. The author's claim that poetry has been around "virtually from the time civilizations invented the written word" is supported by the detail that

a. Beowulf is written in Old English, which is not really in use any longer

b. epic poems told stories about heroes

c. the Renaissance poets tried to copy Greek poets

d. the Mesopotamians are credited with both inventing the word and writing "Epic of Gilgamesh"

22. According to the passage, it can be understood that the word "telling" means

a. speaking

b. significant

c. soothing

d. word**y**

Questions 23 – 27 refer to the following passage.

Passage 8 – Navy Seals

The United States Navy's Sea, Air and Land Teams, commonly known as Navy SEALs, are the U.S. Navy's principle special operations force, and a part of the Naval Special Warfare Command (NSWC) as well as the maritime component of the United States Special Operations Command (USSOCOM).

The unit's acronym ("SEAL") comes from their capacity to operate at sea, in the air, and on land – but it is their ability to work underwater that separates SEALs from most other military units in the world. Navy SEALs are trained and have been deployed in a wide variety of missions, including direct action and special reconnaissance operations, unconventional warfare, foreign internal defence, hostage rescue, counter-terrorism and other missions. All SEALs are members of either the United States Navy or the United States Coast Guard.

In the early morning of May 2, 2011 local time, a team of 40 CIA-led Navy SEALs completed an operation to kill Osama bin Laden in Abbottabad, Pakistan about 35 miles (56 km) from Islamabad, the country's capital. The Navy SEALs were part of the Naval Special Warfare Development Group, previously called "Team 6." President Barack Obama later confirmed the death of bin Laden. The unprecedented media coverage raised the public profile of the SEAL community, particularly the counter-terrorism specialists commonly known as SEAL Team 6. [6]

23. Are Navy SEALs part of USSOCOM?

    a. Yes

    b. No

    c. Only for special operations

    d. No, they are part of the US Navy

24. What separates Navy SEALs from other military units?

    a. Belonging to NSWC

    b. Direct action and special reconnaissance operations

    c. Working underwater

    d. Working for other military units in the world

25. What other military organizations do SEALs belong to?

    a. The US Navy

    b. The Coast Guard

    c. The US Army

    d. The Navy and the Coast Guard

26. What other organization participated in the Bin Laden raid?

    a. The CIA

    b. The US Military

    c. Counter-terrorism specialists

    d. None of the above

27. What is the new name for Team 6?

    a. They were always called Team 6

    b. The counter-terrorism specialists

    c. The Naval Special Warfare Development Group

    d. None of the above

Questions 28 – 33 refer to the following passage.

Passage 9 - Gardening

Gardening for food extends far into prehistory. Ornamental gardens were known in ancient times, a famous example being the Hanging Gardens of Babylon, while ancient Rome had dozens of gardens.

The earliest forms of gardens emerged from the people's need to grow herbs and vegetables. It was only later that rich individuals created gardens for purely decorative purposes.

In ancient Egypt, rich people created ornamental gardens to relax in the shade of the trees. Egyptians believed that gods liked gardens. Commonly, walls surrounded ancient Egyptian gardens with trees planted in rows.

The most popular tree species were date palms, sycamores, fig trees, nut trees, and willows. Besides ornamental gardens, wealthy Egyptians kept vineyards to produce wine.

The Assyrians are also known for their beautiful gardens in what we know today as Iraq. Assyrian gardens were very large, with some of them used for hunting and others as lei-sure gardens. Cypress and palm were the most popular trees in Assyrian gardens. [7]

28. Why did wealthy people in Egypt have gardens?

   a. For food

   b. To relax in the shade

   c. For ornamentation

   d. For hunting

29. What did the Egyptians believe about gardens?

   a. They believed gods loved gardens.

   b. They believed gods hated gardens.

   c. The didn't have any beliefs about gods and Gardens.

   d. They believed gods hated trees.

30. What kinds of trees did the Assyrians like?

   a. The Assyrians liked date palms, sycamores, fig trees, nut trees, and willows.

   b. The Assyrians liked Cypresses and palms.

   c. The Assyrians didn't like trees.

   d. The Assyrians liked hedges and vines.

Section II - Vocabulary.

Choose the word that matches the given definition.

1. VERB To build up or strengthen relative to morals or religion.

    a. Sanctify

    b. Amplify

    c. Edify

    d. Wry

2. NOUN Exit or way out.

    a. Door-jamb

    b. Egress

    c. Regress

    d. Furtherance

3. ADJECTIVE Private, personal.

    a. Confidential

    b. Hysteric

    c. Simplistic

    d. Promissory

4. NOUN Serious criminal offence that is punishable by death or imprisonment above a year.

    a. Trespass

    b. Hampers

    c. Felony

    d. Obligatory

5. VERB To encourage or incite troublesome acts.

   a. Comment

   b. Foment

   c. Integument

   d. Atonement

6. ADJECTIVE Dignified, solemn that is appropriate for a funeral.

   a. Funereal

   b. Prediction

   c. Wailing

   d. Vociferous

7. NOUN Warmth and kindness of disposition.

   a. Seethe

   b. Geniality

   c. Desists

   d. Predicate

8. ADJECTIVE Polite and well mannered.

   a. Chivalrous

   b. Hilarious

   c. Genteel

   d. Governance

9. VERB To encourage, stimulate or incite and provoke.

   a. Push

   b. Force

   c. Threaten

   d. Goad

10. ADJECTIVE Shocking, terrible or wicked.

     a. Pleasantries

     b. Heinous

     c. Shrewd

     d. Provencal

11. NOUN A person of thing that tells or announces the coming of someone or something.

     a. Harbinger

     b. Evasion

     c. Apostate

     d. Coquette

12. ADJECTIVE Similar or identical.

     a. Soluble

     b. Assembly

     c. Conclave

     d. Homologous

13. ADJECTIVE Common, not honorable or noble.

     a. Princely

     b. Ignoble

     c. Shameful

     d. Sham

14. ADJECTIVE Irrelevant not having substance or matter.

     a. Immaterial

     b. Prohibition

     c. Prediction

     d. Brokerage

15. ADJECTIVE Perfect, no faults or errors.

    a. Impeccable

    b. Formidable

    c. Genteel

    d. Disputation

16. VERB Place side by side for contrast or comparison.

    a. Peccadillo

    b. Fallible

    c. Congeal

    d. Juxtapose

17. NOUN Ruling council of a military government.

    a. Sophist

    b. Counsel

    c. Virago

    d. Junta

18. NOUN Someone who takes more time than necessary.

    a. Demagogue

    b. Haggard

    c. Laggard

    d. Investiture

19. ADJECTIVE Lacking enthusiasm, strength or energy.

    a. Hapless

    b. Languid

    c. Ubiquitous

    d. Promiscuous

20. NOUN A person of influence, rank or distinction.

    a. Consummate

    b. Sinister

    c. Accolade

    d. Magnate

21. NOUN A lingering disease or ailment of the human body.

    a. Treatment

    b. Frontal

    c. Malady

    d. Assiduous

22. ADJECTIVE Quick and light in movement.

    a. Quickest

    b. Nimble

    c. Rapacious

    d. Perspicuities

23. ADJECTIVE A loud unpleasant noise.

    a. Nosy

    b. Racket

    c. Ravage

    d. Noisome

24. ADJECTIVE Relating to a wedding or marriage.

    a. Nefarious

    b. Fluctuate

    c. Nuptial

    d. Flatulence

25. ADJECTIVE Open display or apparent.

    a. Ostensible

    b. Complacent

    c. Revealing

    d. Harrowing

26. NOUN A sheet of paper that can be folded into 8 leaves.

    a. Octagon

    b. Harangue

    c. Octavo

    d. Wreckage

27. ADJECTIVE Appearing weak or pale.

    a. Pallid

    b. Palliative

    c. Deviant

    d. Expatiate

28. NOUN A picture or series of pictures representing a continuous scene.

    a. Accolade

    b. Obdurate

    c. Panorama

    d. Personification

29. NOUN A self contradictory statement that can only be true if its false and vice versa.

    a. Inbred

    b. Paradox

    c. Attribute

    d. Fealty

30. ADJECTIVE Often complaining.

    a. Querulous

    b. Complaint

    c. Compound

    d. Vestige

31. NOUN Stillness or pause, something that quiets or represses.

    a. Plausible

    b. Justification

    c. Quietus

    d. Quarantine

32. VERB Question or inquiry.

    a. Cite

    b. Query

    c. Linger

    d. Gibe

33. NOUN A deep narrow valley or gorge cause by running water.

    a. Rumbling

    b. Ravine

    c. Delectable

    d. Distraught

34. VERB Move back or move away.

    a. Implicate

    b. Oscillate

    c. Recede

    d. Meander

35. VERB To become wrinkled.

    a. Sheave

    b. Shrivel

    c. Vernal

    d. Meticulous

36. NOUN A place where people tan hides to make leather.

    a. Shrapnel

    b. Leathery

    c. Tannery

    d. Malleable

37. NOUN An amusing story.

    a. Acronym

    b. Anecdote

    c. Testament

    d. Chaplain

38. ADJECTIVE Complete agreement or harmony.

    a. Ambiguous

    b. Unanimous

    c. Adulate

    d. Incredulous

39. VERB Seize power from another usually by illegitimate means.

    a. Trajectory

    b. Trapeze

    c. Usurp

    d. Benevolence

40. ADJECTIVE Saleable or marketable.

    a. Veneer

    b. Vendible

    c. Venison

    d. Veritable

41. Choose the best definition of importune.

    a. To find an opportunity

    b. To ask all the time.

    c. Cannot find an opportunity

    d. None of the above

42. Choose the best definition of volatile.

    a. Not explosive

    b. Catches fire easily

    c. Does not catch fire

    d. Explosive

43. Choose the best definition of plaintive.

    a. Happy

    b. Mournful

    c. Faint

    d. Plain

44. Choose the best definition of nexus.

    a. A connection

    b. A telephone switch

    c. Part of a computer

    d. None of the above

45. Choose the best definition of conjoin.

    a. A connection

    b. To marry

    c. Weld together

    d. To join together

46. Choose the best definition of petrify.

    a. Turn into a fossil

    b. Turn to stone

    c. Turn into wood

    d. Turn into glass

47. Choose the best definition of inherent.

    a. To receive money in a will

    b. An essential part of

    c. To receive money from a will

    d. None of the above

48. Choose the best definition of torpid.

    a. Fast

    b. Rapid

    c. Sluggish

    d. Violent

49. Choose the best definition of gregarious.

    a. Sociable

    b. Introverted

    c. Large

    d. Solitary

50. Choose the best definition of alloy.

a. To mix with something superior

b. To mix

c. To mix with something inferior

d. To purify

51. Choose the best definition of mollify.

a. To anger

b. To modify

c. To irritate

d. To soothe

52. Choose the best definition of redundant.

a. Backup

b. Necessary repetition

c. Unnecessary repetition

d. No repetition

53. Choose the best definition of bicker.

a. Chat

b. Discuss

c. Argue

d. Debate

54. Choose the best definition of sombre.

a. Gothic

b. Black

c. Serious

d. Evil

55. Choose the best definition of maverick.

a. Rebel

b. Conformist

c. Unconventional

d. Conventional

56. Choose the best definition of tenuous.

a. Strong

b. Tense

c. Firm

d. Weak

57. Choose the best definition of pandemonium.

a. Chaos

b. Orderly

c. Quiet

d. Noisy

58. Choose the best definition of perpetual.

a. Continuous

b. Slowly

c. Over a very long time

d. Motion

59. Choose the best definition of denigrate.

a. Compliment

b. Belittle

c. Praise

d. Admire

60. Choose the best definition of mundane.

   a. Exciting

   b. Continuous

   c. Unforgiving

   d. Ordinary

61. Choose the best definition of bedlam.

   a. In bed

   b. Out of bed

   c. Confusion

   d. Noise

62. Choose the best definition of avert.

   a. To prevent

   b. To look at

   c. To avenge

   d. To facilitate

63. Choose the best definition of dissipate.

   a. Drip

   b. Scatter

   c. Appear

   d. Degenerate

64. Choose the best definition of vexed.

   a. Hexed

   b. Amused

   c. Tickled

   d. Irritated

65. Choose the best definition of gaunt.

   a. Tall

   b. Very thin

   c. Thin

   d. Straight

66. Choose the best definition of epitaph.

   a. Inscription on a tomb

   b. Inscription on a building

   c. Gravestone

   d. None of the above

67. Choose the best definition of oblivion.

   a. Infinity

   b. Far away

   c. Lacking awareness

   d. Blackness

68. Choose the best definition of abhor.

   a. To hate

   b. To give up

   c. To neglect

   d. To throw out

69. Choose the best definition of remuneration.

   a. Give away

   b. Donation

   c. Pay

   d. Fee

70. Choose the best definition of abrasive.

    a. Nasty

    b. Sharp

    c. Prickly

    d. Rough

71. Choose the best definition of engender.

    a. To cause

    b. To create

    c. For both genders

    d. None of the above

72. Choose the best definition of credible.

    a. Not believable

    b. Believable

    c. Sensible

    d. Not sensible

73. Choose the best definition of harbinger.

    a. Indicator

    b. Puzzle

    c. Warning

    d. Danger

74. Choose the best definition of enigma.

    a. Code

    b. Puzzle

    c. Secret

    d. Password

75. Choose the best definition of tardy.

    a. Late

    b. Rude

    c. Polite

    d. Bitter

76. Choose the best definition of blatant.

    a. Not clear

    b. Obvious

    c. Bland

    d. Unusual taste

77. Choose the best definition of tawdry.

    a. Cheap

    b. Expensive

    c. Drab

    d. Thread bare

78. Choose the best definition of gullible.

    a. Does not believe anything

    b. Tells lies

    c. Believes anything

    d. None of the above

79. Choose the best definition of reprieve.

    a. Postponement

    b. Early start

    c. Relief

    d. None of the above

80. Choose the best definition of desist.

    a. Re-start

    b. Stop

    c. Start

    d. Stop for a moment

Answer Key.

SECTION 1 – READING COMPREHENSION.

1. B
We can infer from this passage that sickness from an infectious disease can be easily transmitted from one person to another.

From the passage, "Infectious pathologies are also called communicable diseases or transmissible diseases, due to their potential of transmission from one person or species to another by a replicating agent (as opposed to a toxin)."

2. A
Two other names for infectious pathologies are communicable diseases and transmissible diseases.

From the passage, "Infectious pathologies are also called communicable diseases or transmissible diseases, due to their potential of transmission from one person or species to another by a replicating agent (as opposed to a toxin)."

3. C
Infectivity describes the ability of an organism to enter, survive and multiply in the host. This is taken directly from the passage, and is a definition type question.

Definition type questions can be answered quickly and easily by scanning the passage for the word you are asked to define.

"Infectivity" is an unusual word, so it is quick and easy to scan the passage looking for this word.

4. B
We know an infection is not synonymous with an infectious disease because an infection may not cause important clinical symptoms or impair host function.

5. A
Low blood sugar occurs both in diabetics and healthy adults.

6. B
None of the statements are the author's opinion.

7. A
The author's purpose is to inform.

8. A
The only statement that is **not** a detail is, "A doctor can diagnosis this medical condition by asking the patient questions and testing."

9. C
The cumulus stage of a thunderstorm is the beginning of the thunderstorm.

This is taken directly from the passage, "The first stage of a thunderstorm is the cumulus, or developing stage."

10. D
The passage lists four ways that air is heated. One way is, heat created by water vapor condensing into liquid.

11. A
The sequence of events can be taken from these sentences:

As the moisture carried by the [1] air currents rises, it rapidly cools into liquid drops of water, which appear as cumulus clouds. As the water vapor condenses into liquid, it [2] releases heat, which warms the air. This in turn causes the air to become less dense than the surrounding dry air and [3] rise farther.

12. C
This question tests the reader's vocabulary skills. The uses of the negatives "but" and "less," especially right next to each other, may confuse readers into answering with choices A or D, which list words that are the opposite of "militant." Readers may also be confused by the comparison of healthy people with what is being described as an overly healthy person -- both people are good, but the reader may look for which one is "worse" in the comparison, and therefore stray toward the opposite words.

One key to understanding the meaning of "militant" is to

look at the root; and then easily associate it with "military" and gain a sense of what the word signifies: defense (especially considered that the immune system defends the body). Choice C is correct over B because "militant" is an adjective, just as the words in C are, whereas the words in choice B are nouns.

13. C
This question tests the reader's understanding of function within writing. The other choices are all details included surrounding the quoted text, and may therefore confuse the reader. Choice A somewhat contradicts what is said earlier in the paragraph, which is that tests and treatments are improving, and probably doctors are along with them, but the paragraph doesn't actually mention doctors, and the subject of the question is the medicine. Choice B may seem correct to readers who aren't careful to understand that, while the author does mention the large number of people affected, the author is touching on the realities of living with allergies rather about the likelihood of curing all allergies. Similarly, while the author does mention the "balance" of the body, which is easily associated with "wholesome," the author is not really making an argument and especially is not making an extreme statement that allergy medicines should be outlawed. Again, because the article's tone is on living with allergies, choice C is an appropriate choice that fits with the title and content of the text.

14. B
This question tests the reader's inference skills. The text does not state who is doing the recommending, but the use of the "patients," as well as the general context of the passage, lends itself to the logical partner, "doctors," choice B.

The author does mention the recommendation but doesn't present it as her own (i.e. "I recommend that"), so choice A may be eliminated. It may seem plausible that allergy people with allergies (choice D) may be recommend medicines or products to other people with allergies, but the text does not necessarily support this interaction taking place. Choice C may be selected because the EpiPen is specifically mentioned, but the use of the phrase "such as" when it is introduced is not limiting enough to assume the recommendation is coming from its creators.

15. D

Clouds on Earth are made of water droplets or ice crystals. Clouds in space are made of different materials attracted by gravity.

Choice D is the best answer. Notice also that choice D is the most specific.

16. C

The main idea is the first sentence of the passage; a cloud is a visible mass of droplets or frozen crystals floating in the atmosphere above the surface of the Earth or other planetary body.

The main idea is very often the first sentence of the paragraph.

17. C

Nephology, which is the study of cloud physics.

18. C

This question asks about the process, and gives choices that can be confirmed or eliminated easily.

From the passage, "Dense, deep clouds reflect most light, so they appear white, at least from the top. Cloud droplets scatter light very efficiently, so the farther into a cloud light travels, the weaker it gets. This accounts for the gray or dark appearance at the base of large clouds."

We can eliminate choice A, since water droplets inside the cloud do not reflect light is false.

We can eliminate choice B, since, water droplets outside the cloud reflect light, it appears dark, is false.

Choice C is correct.

19. C

This question tests the reader's summarizing skills. The use of the word "actually" in describing what kind of people poets are, as well as other moments like this, may lead readers to selecting choices B or D, but the author is more information than trying to persuade readers. The author gives no indication that she loves poetry (B) or that people, students specifically (D), should write poems. Choice A is incorrect because the style and content of this paragraph do not match those of a foreword; forewords usually focus on the history or ideas of a specific poem to introduce it more fully and help it stand out against other poems. The author here focuses on several poems and gives broad statements. Instead, she tells a kind of story about poems, giving three very broad time periods in which to discuss them, thereby giving a brief history of poetry, as choice C states.

20. A
This question tests the reader's summarizing skills. Key words in the topic sentences of each of the paragraphs ("oldest," "Renaissance," "modern") should give the reader an idea that the author is moving chronologically. The opening and closing sentence-paragraphs are broad and talk generally. Choice B seems reasonable, but epic poems are mentioned in two paragraphs, eliminating the idea that only new types of poems are used in each paragraph. Choice C is also easily eliminated because the author clearly mentions several different poets, groups of people, and poems. Choice D also seems reasonable, considering that the author does move from older forms of poetry to newer forms, but use of "so (that)" makes this statement false, for the author gives no indication that she is rushing (the paragraphs are about the same size) or that she prefers modern poetry.

21. D
This question tests the reader's attention to detail. The key word is "invented"--it ties together the Mesopotamians, who invented the written word, and the fact that they, as the inventors, also invented and used poetry. The other selections focus on other details mentioned in the passage, such as that the Renaissance's admiration of the Greeks (C) and that Beowulf is in Old English (A). Choice B may seem like an attractive answer because it is unlike the others and because the idea of heroes seems rooted in ancient and early civilizations.

22. B
This question tests the reader's vocabulary and contextualization skills. "Telling" is not an unusual word, but it may be used here in a way that is not familiar to readers, as an adjective rather than a verb in gerund form. Choice A may seem like the obvious answer to a reader looking for a verb to match the use they are familiar with. If the reader understands that the word is being used as an adjective and that choice A is a ploy, they may opt to select choice D, "wordy," but it does not make sense in context. Choice C can be easily eliminated, and doesn't have any connection to the paragraph or passage. "Significant" (B) does make sense contextually, especially in relation to the phrase "give insight" used later in the sentence.

23. A
Navy SEALS are the maritime component of the United States Special Operations Command (USSOCOM).

24. C
Working underwater separates SEALs from other military units. This is taken directly from the passage.

25. D
SEALs also belong to the Navy and the Coast Guard.

26. A
The CIA also participated. From the passage, the raid was conducted by a "team of 40 *CIA-led* Navy SEALS."

27. C
From the passage, "The Navy SEALs were part of the Naval Special Warfare Development Group, previously called 'Team 6.' "

28. B
This question is taken directly from the passage. Scan the passage for the word "Egypt" to find the answer quickly.

29. A
The Egyptians believed gods loved gardens.

30. B
Cypresses and palms were the most popular trees in Assyrian Gardens.

SECTION II - VOCABULARY
ANSWER KEY.

1. C
Edify VERB to instruct or improve morally or intellectually.

2. B
Egress NOUN an exit or way out.

3. A
Confidential ADJECTIVE kept secret within a certain circle of persons; not intended to be known publicly.

4. C
Felony NOUN serious criminal offence that is punishable by death or imprisonment above a year.

5. B
Foment VERB to encourage or incite troublesome acts.

6. A
Funereal ADJECTIVE dignified, solemn that is appropriate for a funeral.

7. B
Geniality NOUN warmth and kindness of disposition.

8. C
Genteel ADJECTIVE polite and well mannered.

9. D
Goad VERB to encourage, stimulate or incite and provoke.

10. B
Heinous ADJECTIVE shocking, terrible or wicked.

11. A
Harbinger NOUN a person of thing that tells or announces the coming of someone or something.

12. D
Homologous ADJECTIVE similar or identical.

13. B
Ignoble ADJECTIVE common, not honorable or noble.

14. A
Immaterial ADJECTIVE irrelevant not having substance or matter.

15. A
Impeccable ADJECTIVE perfect, no faults or errors.

16. D
Juxtapose VERB place side by side for contrast or comparison.

17. D
Junta NOUN ruling council of a military government.

18. C
Laggard NOUN someone who takes more time than necessary.

19. B
Languid ADJECTIVE lacking enthusiasm, strength or energy.

20. D
Magnate NOUN a person of influence, rank or distinction.

21. C
Malady NOUN a lingering disease or ailment of the human body.

22. B
Nimble ADJECTIVE quick and light in movement.

23. B
Racket NOUN a loud noise.

24. C
Nuptial NOUN of or pertaining to wedding and marriage.

25. A
Ostensible ADJECTIVE meant for open display; apparent.

26. C
Octavo NOUN a sheet of paper 7 to 10 inches high and 4.5

to 6 inches wide, the size varying with the large original sheet used to create it. Made by folding the original sheet three times to produce eight leaves.

27. A
Pallid ADJECTIVE appearing weak, pale, or wan.

28. C
Panorama NOUN a picture or series of pictures representing a continuous scene.

29. B
Paradox NOUN a self contradictory statement that can only be true if false and vice versa.

30. A
Querulous ADJECTIVE often complaining; suggesting a complaint in expression; fretful, whining.

31. C
Quietus NOUN a stillness or pause; something that quiets or represses; removal from activity; especially: death.

32. B
Query NOUN question or inquiry.

33. B
Ravine NOUN a deep narrow valley or gorge in the earth's surface worn by running water.

34. C
Recede VERB move back or move away.

35. B
Shrivel VERB to become wrinkled.

36. C
Tannery NOUN a place where people tan hides to make leather.

37. B
Anecdote ADJECTIVE a brief amusing story.

38. B
Unanimous ADJECTIVE complete agreement or harmony.

39. C
Usurp VERB seize power from another usually from illegitimate means.

40. B
Vendible ADJECTIVE saleable or marketable.

41. B
Importune VERB to harass with persistent requests.

42. D
Volatile ADJECTIVE explosive.

43. B
Plaintive ADJECTIVE sorrowful, mournful or melancholic.

44. A
Nexus NOUN a form of connection.

45. D
Conjoin VERB to join together; to unite; to combine.

46. B
Petrify VERB to harden organic matter by permeating with water and depositing dissolved minerals.

47. B
Inherent ADJECTIVE naturally a part or consequence of something.

48. C
Torpid ADJECTIVE lazy, lethargic or apathetic.

49. A
Gregarious ADJECTIVE Describing one who enjoys being in crowds and socializing.

50. C
Alloy VERB to mix or combine; often used of metals.

51. D
Mollify VERB to ease a burden; make less painful; to comfort; soothe.

52. C
Redundant ADJECTIVE repetitive or needlessly wordy.

53. C
Bicker VERB to quarrel in a tiresome, insulting manner.

54. C
Sombre ADJECTIVE dark; gloomy.

55. A
Maverick NOUN showing independence in thoughts or actions.

56. D
Tenuous ADJECTIVE thin in substance or consistency.

57. A
Pandemonium NOUN chaos; tumultuous or lawless violence.

58. A
Perpetual ADJECTIVE continuing uninterrupted.

59. B
Denigrate VERB to treat as worthless; belittle, degrade or disparage.

60. D
Mundane ADJECTIVE ordinary; not new.

61. C
Bedlam NOUN a place or situation of chaotic uproar, and where confusion prevails.

62. A
Avert VERB to ward off, or prevent, the occurrence or effects of.

63. B
Dissipate VERB to drive away; scatter.
64. D
Vexed VERB annoyed, irritated or distressed.

65. B
Gaunt ADJECTIVE lean, angular and bony.

66. A
Epitaph NOUN an inscription on a gravestone in memory of the deceased.

67. C
Oblivion NOUN the state of forgetfulness or distraction.

68. A
Abhor VERB to regard with horror or detestation.

69. C
Remuneration NOUN a payment for work done; wages, salary, emolument.

70. D
Abrasive ADJECTIVE being rough and coarse in manner or disposition.

71. B
Engender VERB to give existence to; to produce.

72. B
Credible ADJECTIVE believable or plausible.

73. A
Harbinger NOUN a person or thing that foreshadows or foretells the coming of someone or something.

74. B
Enigma NOUN something puzzling, mysterious or inexplicable.

75. A
Tardy NOUN late, overdue or delayed.

76. B
Blatant ADJECTIVE obvious; on show.

77. A
Tawdry ADJECTIVE cheap and gaudy; showy.

78. C
Gullible ADJECTIVE easily deceived or duped; naïve, easily cheated or fooled.

79. A
Reprieve ADJECTIVE The cancellation or postponement of a punishment.

80. B
Desist VERB to cease to proceed or act; to stop; to forbear. [4]

Practice Test Questions Set 2

Section I – Reading Comprehension

Questions: 30

Section II – Vocabulary

Questions: 80

This set of practice test questions presents questions that represent the type of question you should expect to find on the Nelson Denny. However, they are not intended to match exactly what is on the NDRT.

For the best results, take these practice questions as if it were the real exam. Set aside time when you will not be disturbed, and a location that is quiet and free of distractions. Read the instructions carefully, read each question carefully, and answer to the best of your ability.

Use the bubble answer sheets provided. When you have completed the practice questions, check your answer against the Answer Key and read the explanation provided.

Reading Comprehension Answer Sheet.

1. (A) (B) (C) (D)   11. (A) (B) (C) (D)   21. (A) (B) (C) (D)

2. (A) (B) (C) (D)   12. (A) (B) (C) (D)   22. (A) (B) (C) (D)

3. (A) (B) (C) (D)   13. (A) (B) (C) (D)   23. (A) (B) (C) (D)

4. (A) (B) (C) (D)   14. (A) (B) (C) (D)   24. (A) (B) (C) (D)

5. (A) (B) (C) (D)   15. (A) (B) (C) (D)   25. (A) (B) (C) (D)

6. (A) (B) (C) (D)   16. (A) (B) (C) (D)   26. (A) (B) (C) (D)

7. (A) (B) (C) (D)   17. (A) (B) (C) (D)   27. (A) (B) (C) (D)

8. (A) (B) (C) (D)   18. (A) (B) (C) (D)   28. (A) (B) (C) (D)

9. (A) (B) (C) (D)   19. (A) (B) (C) (D)   29. (A) (B) (C) (D)

10. (A) (B) (C) (D)   20. (A) (B) (C) (D)   30. (A) (B) (C) (D)

Nelson Denny Practice!

Vocabulary Answer Sheet

1. (A)(B)(C)(D)	21. (A)(B)(C)(D)	41. (A)(B)(C)(D)	61. (A)(B)(C)(D)
2. (A)(B)(C)(D)	22. (A)(B)(C)(D)	42. (A)(B)(C)(D)	62. (A)(B)(C)(D)
3. (A)(B)(C)(D)	23. (A)(B)(C)(D)	43. (A)(B)(C)(D)	63. (A)(B)(C)(D)
4. (A)(B)(C)(D)	24. (A)(B)(C)(D)	44. (A)(B)(C)(D)	64. (A)(B)(C)(D)
5. (A)(B)(C)(D)	25. (A)(B)(C)(D)	45. (A)(B)(C)(D)	65. (A)(B)(C)(D)
6. (A)(B)(C)(D)	26. (A)(B)(C)(D)	46. (A)(B)(C)(D)	66. (A)(B)(C)(D)
7. (A)(B)(C)(D)	27. (A)(B)(C)(D)	47. (A)(B)(C)(D)	67. (A)(B)(C)(D)
8. (A)(B)(C)(D)	28. (A)(B)(C)(D)	48. (A)(B)(C)(D)	68. (A)(B)(C)(D)
9. (A)(B)(C)(D)	29. (A)(B)(C)(D)	49. (A)(B)(C)(D)	69. (A)(B)(C)(D)
10. (A)(B)(C)(D)	30. (A)(B)(C)(D)	50. (A)(B)(C)(D)	70. (A)(B)(C)(D)
11. (A)(B)(C)(D)	31. (A)(B)(C)(D)	51. (A)(B)(C)(D)	71. (A)(B)(C)(D)
12. (A)(B)(C)(D)	32. (A)(B)(C)(D)	52. (A)(B)(C)(D)	72. (A)(B)(C)(D)
13. (A)(B)(C)(D)	33. (A)(B)(C)(D)	53. (A)(B)(C)(D)	73. (A)(B)(C)(D)
14. (A)(B)(C)(D)	34. (A)(B)(C)(D)	54. (A)(B)(C)(D)	74. (A)(B)(C)(D)
15. (A)(B)(C)(D)	35. (A)(B)(C)(D)	55. (A)(B)(C)(D)	75. (A)(B)(C)(D)
16. (A)(B)(C)(D)	36. (A)(B)(C)(D)	56. (A)(B)(C)(D)	76. (A)(B)(C)(D)
17. (A)(B)(C)(D)	37. (A)(B)(C)(D)	57. (A)(B)(C)(D)	77. (A)(B)(C)(D)
18. (A)(B)(C)(D)	38. (A)(B)(C)(D)	58. (A)(B)(C)(D)	78. (A)(B)(C)(D)
19. (A)(B)(C)(D)	39. (A)(B)(C)(D)	59. (A)(B)(C)(D)	79. (A)(B)(C)(D)
20. (A)(B)(C)(D)	40. (A)(B)(C)(D)	60. (A)(B)(C)(D)	80. (A)(B)(C)(D)

Section I – Reading Comprehension.

Questions 1-4 refer to the following passage.

Passage 1 - The Respiratory System

The respiratory system's function is to allow oxygen exchange through all parts of the body. The anatomy or structure of the exchange system, and the uses of the exchanged gases, varies depending on the organism. In humans and other mammals, for example, the anatomical features of the respiratory system include airways, lungs, and the respiratory muscles. Molecules of oxygen and carbon dioxide are passively exchanged, by diffusion, between the gaseous external environment and the blood. This exchange process occurs in the alveolar region of the lungs.

Other animals, such as insects, have respiratory systems with very simple anatomical features, and in amphibians even the skin plays a vital role in gas exchange. Plants also have respiratory systems but the direction of gas exchange can be opposite to that of animals.

The respiratory system can also be divided into physiological, or functional, zones. These include the conducting zone (the region for gas transport from the outside atmosphere to just above the alveoli), the transitional zone, and the respiratory zone (the alveolar region where gas exchange occurs). [8]

1. What can we infer from the first paragraph in this passage?

    a.   Human and mammal respiratory systems are the same.

    b.   The lungs are an important part of the respiratory system.

    c.   The respiratory system varies in different mammals.

    d.   Oxygen and carbon dioxide are passive exchanged by the respiratory system.

2. What is the process by which molecules of oxygen and carbon dioxide are passively exchanged?

    a. Transfusion

    b. Affusion

    c. Diffusion

    d. Respiratory confusion

3. What organ plays an important role in gas exchange in amphibians?

    a. The skin

    b. The lungs

    c. The gills

    d. The mouth

4. What are the three physiological zones of the respiratory system?

    a. Conducting, transitional, respiratory zones

    b. Redacting, transitional, circulatory zones

    c. Conducting, circulatory, inhibiting zones

    d. Transitional, inhibiting, conducting zones

Questions 5 - 8 refer to the following passage.

The Civil War

The Civil War began on April 12, 1861. The first shots of the Civil War were fired in Fort Sumter, South Carolina. Note that even though more American lives were lost in the Civil War than in any other war, not one person died on that first day. The war began because eleven Southern states seceded from the Union and tried to start their own government, The Confederate States of America.

Why did the states secede? The issue of slavery was a primary cause of the Civil War. The eleven southern states relied heavily on their slaves to foster their farming and plantation lifestyles. The northern states, many of whom had already abolished slavery, did not feel that the southern states should have slaves. The north wanted to free all the slaves and President Lincoln's goal was to both end slavery and preserve the Union. He had Congress declare war on the Confederacy on April 14, 1862. For four long, blood soaked years, the North and South fought.

From 1861 to mid 1863, it seemed as if the South would win this war. However, on July 1, 1863, an epic three day battle was waged on a field in Gettysburg, Pennsylvania. Gettysburg is remembered for being the bloodiest battle in American history. At the end of the three days, the North turned the tide of the war in their favor.   The North then went onto dominate the South for the remainder of the war. Most well remembered might be General Sherman's "March to The Sea," where he famously led the Union Army through Georgia and the Carolinas, burning and destroying everything in their path.

In 1865, the Union army invaded and captured the Confederate capital of Richmond Virginia. Robert E. Lee, leader of the Confederacy surrendered to General Ulysses S. Grant, leader of the Union forces, on April 9, 1865. The Civil War was over and the Union was preserved.

5. What does the word secede most nearly mean?

    a. To break away from

    b. To accomplish

    c. To join

    d. To lose

6. Which of the following statements summarizes a FACT from the passage?

a. Congress declared war and then the Battle of Fort Sumter began.

b. Congress declared war after shots were fired at Fort Sumter.

c. President Lincoln was pro slavery

d. President Lincoln was at Fort Sumter with Congress

7. Which event finally led the Confederacy to surrender?

a. The battle of Gettysburg

b. The battle of Bull Run

c. The invasion of the confederate capital of Richmond

d. Sherman's March to the Sea

8. The word abolish as used in this passage most nearly means?

a. To ban

b. To polish

c. To support

d. To destroy

Questions 9 – 11 refer to the following passage.

Passage 2 – Mythology

The main characters in myths are usually gods or supernatural heroes. As sacred stories, rulers and priests have traditionally endorsed their myths and as a result, myths have a close link with religion and politics. In the society where a myth originates, the natives believe the myth is a true account of the remote past. In fact, many societies have two categories of traditional narrative—(1) "true stories," or myths, and (2) "false stories," or fables.

Myths generally take place during a primordial age, when

the world was still young, prior to achieving its current form. These stories explain how the world gained its current form and why the culture developed its customs, institutions, and taboos. Closely related to myth are legend and folktale. Myths, legends, and folktales are different types of traditional stories. Unlike myths, folktales can take place at any time and any place, and the natives do not usually consider them true or sacred. Legends, on the other hand, are similar to myths in that many people have traditionally considered them true. Legends take place in a more recent time, when the world was much as it is today. In addition, legends generally feature humans as their main characters, whereas myths have superhuman characters. [9]

9. We can infer from this passage that

a. Folktales took place in a time far past, before civilization covered the earth.

b. Humankind uses myth to explain how the world was created.

c. Myths revolve around gods or supernatural beings; the local community usually accepts these stories as not true.

d. The only difference between a myth and a legend is the time setting of the story.

10. The main purpose of this passage is

a. To distinguish between many types of traditional stories, and explain the background of some traditional story categories.

b. To determine whether myths and legends might be true accounts of history.

c. To show the importance of folktales how these traditional stories made life more bearable in harder times.

d. None of the Above.

11. How are folktales different from myths?

a. Folktales and myth are the same.

b. Folktales are not true and generally not sacred and take place anytime.

c. Myths are not true and generally not sacred and take place anytime.

d. Folktales explained the formation of the world and myths do not.

Questions 12 refers to the following table of contents.

Getting Started

12. Based on the partial table of contents above, what is this book about?

a. How to answer multiple choice questions

b. Different types of multiple choice questions

c. How to write a test

d. None of the above

Questions 13 - 16 refer to the following passage.

Passage 3 – Myths, Legend and Folklore

Cultural historians draw a distinction between myth, legend and folktale simply as a way to group traditional stories. However, in many cultures, drawing a sharp line between myths and legends is not that simple. Instead of dividing their traditional stories into myths, legends, and folktales, some cultures divide them into two categories. The first category roughly corresponds to folktales, and the second is one that combines myths and legends. Similarly, we can not always separate myths from folktales. One society might consider a story true, making it a myth. Another society may believe the story is fiction, which makes it a folktale. In fact, when a myth loses its status as part of a religious system, it often takes on traits more typical of folktales, with its formerly divine characters now appearing as human heroes, giants, or fairies. Myth, legend, and folktale are only a few of the categories of traditional stories. Other categories include anecdotes and some kinds of jokes. Traditional stories, in turn, are only one category within the larger category of folklore, which also includes items such as gestures, costumes, and music. [9]

13. The main idea of this passage is that

a. Myths, fables, and folktales are not the same thing, and each describes a specific type of story.

b. Traditional stories can be categorized in different ways by different people.

c. Cultures use myths for religious purposes, and when this is no longer true, the people forget and discard these myths.

d. Myths can never become folk tales, because one is true, and the other is false.

14. The terms myth and legend are

a. Categories that are synonymous with true and false.

b. Categories that group traditional stories according to certain characteristics.

c. Interchangeable, because both terms mean a story that is passed down from generation to generation.

d. Meant to distinguish between a story that involves a hero and a cultural message and a story meant only to entertain.

15. Traditional story categories not only include myths and legends, but

a. Can also include gestures, since some cultures passed these down before the written and spoken word.

b. In addition, folklore refers to stories involving fables and fairy tales.

c. These story categories can also include folk music and traditional dress.

d. Traditional stories themselves are a part of the larger category of folklore, which may also include costumes, gestures, and music.

16. This passage shows that

a. There is a distinct difference between a myth and a legend, although both are folktales.

b. Myths are folktales, but folktales are not myths.

c. Myths, legends, and folktales play an important part in tradition and the past, and are a rich and colorful part of history.

d. Most cultures consider myths to be true.

Questions 17 - 21 refer to the following passage.

A Day That Will Live in Infamy! Attack on Pearl Harbor

In 1941, the world was at war. The United States was trying very hard to keep itself out of the conflict. In Europe, the countries of Germany and Italy had formed an alliance to expand their land and territory. Germany had already taken over Poland, Denmark, and parts of France. They were heading next toward England and due to all the fighting in Europe, there were battles taking place as far south as North Africa, where the German and Italian armies were fighting the British.

This got even worse when the Asian nation of Japan formed an alliance with Germany and Italy. Together, the three countries called themselves, the AXIS. Now, the war was in the Pacific as well as in Europe and Northern Africa. Many Americans felt that perhaps now was the time for the United States to join with its ally, Great Britain and stop the Axis from taking over more regions of the world.

In 1941, Franklin Roosevelt was President of the United States. His fear at the time was that Japan would try to take over many countries in Asia. He did not want to see that happen, so he moved some of the United States warships that had been stationed in San Diego, to the military base at Pearl Harbor, in Honolulu, Hawaii.

Japan quietly plotted their attack. They waited until the early hours of the morning on Sunday, December 7, 1941. Then, 350 Japanese war plans began to drop bombs on the U.S. ships at Pearl Harbor.

The first bombs fell at 7:48 am and a mere 90 minutes later, the attack was over. Pearl Harbor was decimated. 8 battle-ships were damaged. Eleven ships were sunk and 300 U.S. planes were destroyed. Most devastating was the loss of life 2,400 U.S. military members was killed in the attack and 1, 282 were injured.

President Roosevelt addressed the country via the radio and said "Today is a day that will live in infamy." He asked Congress to declare war on Japan. War was declared on Japan on December 8th and on Germany and Italy on December 11th. The United States had entered World War Two.

17. After reading the passage, what can we infer the word infamy means?

    a. Famous

    b. Remembered in a good way

    c. Remembered in a bad way

    d. Easily forgotten

18. What three countries formed the Axis?

    a. Italy, England, Germany

    b. United States, England, Italy

    c. Germany, Japan, Italy

    d. Germany, Japan, United States

19. What do you think was President Roosevelt's reason for moving warships to Pearl Harbor?

    a. He feared Japan would bomb San Diego

    b. He knew Japan was going to attack Pearl Harbor

    c. He was planning to attack Japan

    d. He wanted to try and protect Asian countries from Japanese takeover

20. Why do you think Japan chose a Sunday morning at 7:48 am for their attack?

    a. They knew the military slept late

    b. There is a law against bombing countries on a Sunday

    c. They wanted the attack to catch people by surprise

    d. That was the only free time they had to attack.

Questions 21 - 24 refer to the following passage.

The Winged Victory of Samothrace: the Statue of the Gods

Students who read about the "Winged Victory of Samothrace" probably won't be able to picture what this statue looks like. However, almost anyone who knows a little about statues will recognize it when they see it: it is the statue of a winged woman who does not have arms or a head. Even the most famous pieces of art may be recognized by sight but not by name.

This iconic statue is of the Greek goddess Nike, who represented victory and was called Victoria by the Romans. The statue is sometimes called the "Nike of Samothrace". She was often displayed in Greek art as driving a chariot, and her speed or efficiency with the chariot may be what her wings symbolize. It is said that the statue was created around 200 BCE to celebrate a battle that was won at sea. Archaeologists and art historians believe the statue may have originally been part of a temple or other building, even one of the most important temples, Megaloi Theoi, just as many statues were used during that time.

"Winged Victory" does indeed appear to have had arms and a head when it was originally created, and it is unclear why they were removed or lost. Indeed, they have never been discovered, even with all the excavation that has taken place. Many speculate that one of her arms was raised and put to her mouth, as though she was shouting or calling out, which is consistent with the idea of her as a war figure. If the missing pieces were ever to be found, they might give Greek and art historians more of an idea of what Nike represented or how the statue was used.

Learning about pieces of art through details like these can help students remember time frames or locations, as well as learn about the people who occupied them.

21. The author's title says the statue is "of the Gods" because

a. the statue is very beautiful and even a god would find it beautiful

b. the statue is of a Greek goddess, and gods were of primary importance to the Greek

c. Nike lead the gods into war

d. the statues were used at the temple of the gods and so it belonged to them

22. The third paragraph states that

a. the statue is related to war and was probably broken apart by foreign soldiers

b. the arms and head of the statue cannot be found because all the excavation has taken place

c. speculations have been made about what the entire statue looked like and what it symbolized

d. the statue has no arms or head because the sculptor lost them

23. The author's main purpose in writing this passage is to

a. demonstrate that art and culture are related and one can teach us about the other

b. persuade readers to become archeologists and find the missing pieces of the statue

c. teach readers about the Greek goddess Nike

d. to teach readers the name of a statue they probably recognize

24. The author specifies the indirect audience as "students" because

a. it is probably a student who is taking this test

b. most young people don't know much about art yet and most young people are students

c. students read more than people who are not students

d. the passage is based on a discussion of what we can learn about culture from art

Questions 25 - 27 refer to the following passage.

Lowest Price Guarantee

Get it for less. Guaranteed!

ABC Electric will beat any advertised price by 10% of the difference.

1) If you find a lower advertised price, we will beat it by 10% of the difference.

2) If you find a lower advertised price within 30 days* of your purchase we will beat it by 10% of the difference.

3) If our own price is reduced within 30 days* of your purchase, bring in your receipt and we will refund the difference.

*14 days for computers, monitors, printers, laptops, tablets, cellular & wireless devices, home security products, projectors, camcorders, digital cameras, radar detectors, portable DVD players, DJ and pro-audio equipment, and air conditioners.

25. I bought a radar detector 15 days ago and saw an ad for the same model only cheaper. Can I get 10% of the difference refunded?

a. Yes. Since it is less than 30 days, you can get 10% of the difference refunded.

b. No. Since it is more than 14 days, you cannot get 10% of the difference re-funded.

c. It depends on the cashier.

d. Yes. You can get the difference refunded.

26. I bought a flat-screen TV for $500 10 days ago and found an advertisement for the same TV, at another store, on sale for $400. How much will ABC refund under this guarantee?

a. $100

b. $110

c. $10

d. $400

27. What is the purpose of this passage?

    a. To inform

    b. To educate

    c. To persuade

    d. To entertain

Questions 28 - 30 refer to the following passage.

Ways Characters Communicate in Theater

Playwrights give their characters voices in a way that gives depth and added meaning to what happens on stage during their play. There are different types of speech in scripts that allow characters to talk with themselves, with other characters, and even with the audience.

It is very unique to theater that characters may talk "to themselves." When characters do this, the speech they give is called a soliloquy. Soliloquies are usually poetic, introspective, moving, and can tell audience members about the feelings, motivations, or suspicions of an individual character without that character having to reveal them to other characters on stage. "To be or not to be" is a famous soliloquy given by Hamlet as he considers difficult but important themes, such as life and death.

The most common type of communication in plays is when one character is speaking to another or a group of other characters. This is generally called dialogue, but can also be called monologue if one character speaks without being interrupted for a long time. It is not necessarily the most important type of communication, but it is the most common because the plot of the play cannot really progress without it.

Lastly, and most unique to theater (although it has been used somewhat in film) is when a character speaks directly to the audience. This is called an aside, and scripts usually specifically direct actors to do this. Asides are usually comical, an inside joke between the character and the audience, and very short. The actor will usually face the audience when delivering them, even if it's for a moment, so the audience can recognize this move as an aside.

All three of these types of communication are important to the art of theater, and have been perfected by famous playwrights like Shakespeare. Understanding these types of communication can help an audience member grasp what is artful about the script and action of a play.

28. According to the passage, characters in plays communicate to

    a. move the plot forward

    b. show the private thoughts and feelings of one character

    c. make the audience laugh

    d. add beauty and artistry to the play

29. When Hamlet delivers "To be or not to be", he can most likely be described as

    a. solitary

    b. thoughtful

    c. dramatic

    d. hopeless

30. The author uses parentheses to punctuate "although it has been used somewhat in film"

    a. to show that films are less important

    b. instead of using commas so that the sentence is not interrupted

    c. because parenthesis help separate details that are not as important

    d. to show that films are not as artistic

Section II - Vocabulary.

Choose the best word for the given definition.

1. NOUN Use of too many words.

    a. Verbiage

    b. Outspoken

    c. Inveigh

    d. Precarious

2. NOUN An aide or assistant.

    a. Attache

    b. Influx

    c. Mien

    d. Knoll

3. VERB To cause or inflict especially related to harm or injury.

    a. Wreak

    b. Mandible

    c. Tremulous

    d. Juxtapose

4. ADJECTIVE Foolish, without understanding.

    a. Coinage

    b. Witless

    c. Distinctive

    d. Nullify

5. ADJECTIVE Strong fear of strangers.

    a. Xenophobia

    b. Agoraphobia

    c. Frightful

    d. Genteel

6. NOUN Highest point, highest state or peak.

    a. Towering

    b. Flickers

    c. Zenith

    d. Grouse

7. NOUN Light wind or gentle breeze.

    a. Sea-breeze

    b. Scuttle

    c. Zephyr

    d. Freight

8. NOUN Self evident or clear obvious truth.

    a. Truism

    b. Catharsis

    c. Libertine

    d. Tractable

9. ADJECTIVE Beyond what is obvious or evident.

    a. Ulterior

    b. Sybarite

    c. Torsion

    d. Trenchant

10. ADJECTIVE Tasteless or bland.

    a. Obstinate
    b. Morose
    c. Inculpate
    d. Vapid

11. NOUN homeless child or stray.

    a. Elegy
    b. Waif
    c. Martyr
    d. Palaver

12. VERB Complaint or criticism.

    a. Obsequies
    b. Whine
    c. Opprobrious
    d. Panacea

13. NOUN Subordinate of lesser rank or authority.

    a. Palliate
    b. Plebeian
    c. Underling
    d. Expiate

14. NOUN A young animal that is between 1 and 2 years.

    a. Yearling
    b. Rogue
    c. Gnostic
    d. Billet

15. NOUN Lush green vegetation.

    a. Coquette

    b. Verdure

    c. Ennui

    d. Lugubrious

16. NOUN A person who is very passionate and fanatic about his specific objectives or beliefs.

    a. Plebeian

    b. Zealot

    c. Progenitor

    d. Iconoclast

17. NOUN Dizziness.

    a. Indolence

    b. Percipient

    c. Vertigo

    d. Tenacious

18. ADJECTIVE Obvious or easy to notice.

    a. Important

    b. Conspicuous

    c. Beautiful

    d. Convincing

19. NOUN Disposition to do good.

    a. Happiness

    b. Courage

    c. Kindness

    d. Benevolence

20. ADJECTIVE Full of energy; exuberant; noisy.

a. Boisterous
b. Soft
c. Gentle
d. Warm

21. VERB To fondle.

a. Hold
b. Caress
c. Facilitate
d. Neuter

22. ADJECTIVE Outstanding in importance.

a. Momentous
b. Spurious
c. Extraordinary
d. Secede

23. NOUN An opponent or enemy.

a. Antagonist
b. Protagonist
c. Sophist
d. Pugilist

24. NOUN A keepsake; an object kept as a reminder of a place or event.

a. Monument
b. Memento
c. Recurrence
d. Catharsis

25. ADJECTIVE Producing harm in a stealthy, often gradual, manner.

    a. Adulterate

    b. Acquiesce

    c. Insidious

    d. Deceitful

26. NOUN A route or proposed route of a journey.

    a. Schedule

    b. Guidebook

    c. Itinerary

    d. Diary

27. ADJECTIVE Dignified.

    a. Rich

    b. Noble

    c. Gallant

    d. Illustrious

28. ADJECTIVE Sharp deep cutting or biting.

    a. Trenchant

    b. Apprehensible

    c. Bulbous

    d. Invidious

29. VERB To kiss or related to kissing.

    a. Knead

    b. Defalcate

    c. Upbraid

    d. Osculate

30. NOUN Change or alteration.

    a. Mutation

    b. Veracity

    c. Oration

    d. Facet

31. ADJECTIVE Flexible or plaint.

    a. Facile

    b. Lithe

    c. Misanthropic

    d. Prescient

32. VERB To express displeasure or indignation.

    a. Sanction

    b. Resent

    c. Venerate

    d. Cull

33. ADJECTIVE Fat, plump and overweight.

    a. Chubby

    b. Corrigible

    c. Heathenish

    d. Peccant

34. ADJECTIVE Fearful or timid.

    a. Skittish

    b. Pervious

    c. Prefatory

    d. Reparable

35. ADJECTIVE Harsh or rough sounding.

a. Rambunctious

b. Unctuous

c. Exorbitant

d. Cardinal

36. ADJECTIVE Indicating or expressing a cause.

a. Averse

b. Nominal

c. Reprehensible

d. Causal

37. ADJECTIVE Able to be kept under restraint or control.

a. Rampant

b. Repressible

c. Exigent

d. Exemplary

38. ADJECTIVE Living both on land and in water.

a. Amicable

b. Fervid

c. Amphibious

d. Frigid

39. VERB To imbue with life or animation.

a. Grapple

b. Galvanize

c. Luxuriate

d. Mete

40. NOUN A slight degree of difference in anything perceptible to the sense of the mind.

    a. Nuance

    b. Omission

    c. Peerage

    d. Petulance

41. Choose the best definition of obfuscate.

    a. Deliberately make noisy

    b. Deliberately make difficult

    c. Deliberately make quiet

    d. Talk about for a long time

42. Choose the best definition of plethora.

    a. Too many

    b. Too few

    c. A lot

    d. A few

43. Choose the best definition of laceration.

    a. A stripe

    b. A mark

    c. A scratch

    d. A cut

44. Choose the best definition of enshroud.

    a. Hold up

    b. Cover

    c. Wear

    d. Take away

45. Choose the best definition of hasten.

    a. To hurry

    b. To climb

    c. To fasten

    d. To worry

46. Choose the best definition of pliable.

    a. Rigid

    b. Fixable

    c. Bend able

    d. None of the Above

47. Choose the best definition of blithe.

    a. Skinny

    b. Tall

    c. Carefree

    d. Lithe

48. Choose the best definition of rescind.

    a. To take back

    b. To give away

    c. To enforce

    d. To straighten

49. Choose the best definition of headstrong.

    a. Does not listen

    b. Stubborn

    c. Willing

    d. To disbelieve

50. Choose the best definition of oblique.

    a. Direct

    b. Indirect

    c. Sharp

    d. Straight

51. Choose the best definition of temper.

    a. To make worse

    b. To aggravate

    c. To soften

    d. None of the Above

52. Choose the best definition of cryptic.

    a. Building in a graveyard

    b. Difficult to understand

    c. Printed in code

    d. None of the above

53. Choose the best definition of curtail.

    a. To cut short

    b. To arrive early

    c. To lengthen

    d. To give back

54. Choose the best definition of heed.

    a. To ignore

    b. To listen

    c. To advise

    d. To pay

55. Choose the best definition of oblivious.

a. Far Away

b. Believable

c. Unbelievable

d. Totally unaware

56. Choose the best definition of podium.

a. Speaker

b. Raised platform

c. Brief lecture

d. None of the above

57. Choose the best definition of boorish.

a. Bad tempered

b. Bad mannered

c. Bad looking

d. Bad smelling

58. Choose the best definition of heresy.

a. Against the orthodox opinion

b. Same as the orthodox opinion

c. An unusual opinion

d. To have no opinion

59. Choose the best definition of respite.

a. A drink

b. Intermission

c. A rest stop on highways

d. An interval

60. Choose the best definition of regicide.

a. To endow or furnish with requisite ability

b. Killing a king

c. Disposed to seize by violence or by unlawful or greedy methods

d. To refresh after labor

61. Choose the best definition of salient.

a. To make light by fermentation, as dough

b. Not stringent or energetic

c. Negligible

d. Worthy of note or relevant

62. Choose the best definition of sedentary.

a. Yellowing of the skin

b. Not moving or sitting in one a place

c. To wander from place to place

d. Perplexity

63. Choose the best definition of sedulous.

a. The support on or against which a lever rests

b. Dedicated and diligent

c. To oppose with an equal force

d. The branch of medical science that relates to improving health

64. Choose the best definition of tincture.

a. Alcoholic drink with plant extract used for medicine

b. An artificial trance-sleep

c. A special medicinal drink made by mixing water with plant extracts

d. The point of puncture

65. Choose the best definition of truism.

a. A comparison which directs the mind to the representative object itself

b. Self evident or clear obvious truth

c. A statement that is true but that can hardly be proved

d. False statements

66. Choose the best definition of mutation.

a. To utter with a loud and vehement voice

b. Change or alteration

c. An act or exercise of will

d. To cause to be one

67. Choose the best definition of alchemy.

a. Small in size

b. Change metal into gold

c. Flexible or pliant

d. Fake

68. Choose the best definition of benchmark.

a. A standard of measure

b. To cause boredom

c. Clumsy

d. Strong feelings of love

69. Choose the best definition of pudgy.

a. To draw general inferences

b. Fat, plump and overweight

c. Permanence

d. Spoilt or bad condition

70. Choose the best definition of timorous.

    a. Fearful or timid

    b. Third from last

    c. Reprove; accuse; condemn

    d. Happy

71. Choose the best definition of raucous.

    a. Pedantic; academic; for teaching

    b. Contemptuous, scornful

    c. Not essential under the circumstances

    d. Harsh or rough sounding

72. Choose the best definition of abet.

    a. To aid, help

    b. To reject

    c. To kidnap

    d. To fly

73. Choose the best definition of adorn.

    a. To decorate

    b. To dismantle

    c. To stick something to

    d. To outline vaguely

74. Choose the best definition of allege.

    a. To summarize

    b. To re-distribute

    c. To say without proof

    d. To increase

75. Choose the best definition of nomadic.

a. Happening at night
b. Wandering
c. Unyielding
d. Foreboding

76. Choose the best definition of appease.

a. To take, or make use of
b. Shock or disgust
c. To take without justification
d. To calm or satisfy

77. Choose the best definition of opulent.

a. Ostentatiously rich and lavish
b. Appearing as such
c. Greatest in importance
d. Easily understood

78. Choose the best definition of perfunctory.

a. With little interest or enthusiasm
b. Flippant or bold
c. Difficult to understand
d. Skillful

79. Choose the best definition of flout.

a. To give up
b. To disregard or disobey
c. To absorb or engross
d. To make an impression

80. Choose the best definition of indefatigable.

   a. Incapable of defeat

   b. Not changeable

   c. Assumed to be true

   d. Talkative or wordy

Answer Key

SECTION I - READING COMPREHENSION

1. B
We can infer an important part of the respiratory system are the lungs. From the passage, "Molecules of oxygen and carbon dioxide are passively exchanged, by diffusion, between the gaseous external environment and the blood. This exchange process occurs in the alveolar region of the lungs."

Therefore, one of the primary functions for the respiratory system is the exchange of oxygen and carbon dioxide, and this process occurs in the lungs. We can therefore infer that the lungs are an important part of the respiratory system.

2. C
The process by which molecules of oxygen and carbon dioxide are passively exchanged is diffusion.

This is a definition type question. Scan the passage for references to "oxygen," "carbon dioxide," or "exchanged."

3. A
The organ that plays an important role in gas exchange in amphibians is the skin.

Scan the passage for references to "amphibians," and find the answer.

4. A
The three physiological zones of the respiratory system are Conducting, transitional, respiratory zones.

5. A
Secede most nearly means to break away from because the 11 states wanted to leave the United States and form their own country.

Choice B is incorrect because the states were not accomplishing anything. Choice C is incorrect because the states were trying to leave the USA not join it. Choice D is incorrect because the states seceded before they lost the war.

6. B

Look at the dates in the passage. The shots were fired on April 12 and Congress declared war on April 14.

Choice A is incorrect because the dates show clearly which happened first. Choice C is incorrect because the passage states that Lincoln was against slavery. Choice D is incorrect because it never mentions who was or was not at Fort Sumter.

7. C

The passage clearly states that Lee surrendered to Grant after the capture of the capital of the Confederacy, which is Richmond. Choice A is incorrect because the war continued for 2 years after Gettysburg.

Choice B is incorrect because that battle is never mentioned in the passage. Choice D is incorrect because the capture of the capital occurred after the march to the sea.

8. A

When the passage said that the North had abolished slavery, it implies that slaves were no longer allowed to be had in the North. In essence slavery was banned.

Choice B is incorrect because it makes no sense relative to the context of the passage. Choice C is incorrect because we know the North was fighting against slavery, not for it. Choice D is incorrect because slavery is not a tangible thing that can be destroyed. It is a practice that had to be outlawed or banned.

9. B

The first paragraph tells us that myths are a true account of the remote past.

The second paragraph tells us that, "myths generally take place during a primordial age, when the world was still young, prior to achieving its current form."

Putting these two together, we can infer that humankind used myth to explain how the world was created.

10. A
This passage is about different types of stories. First, the passage explains myths, and then compares other types of stories to myths.

11. B
From the passage, "Unlike myths, folktales can take place at any time and any place, and the natives do not usually consider them true or sacred."

12. A
Based on the partial table of contents, this book is most likely about how to answer multiple choice.

13. B
This passage describes the different categories for traditional stories. The other choices are facts from the passage, not the main idea of the passage. The main idea of a passage will always be the most general statement. For example, choice A, Myths, fables, and folktales are not the same thing, and each describes a specific type of story. This is a true statement from the passage, but not the main idea of the passage, since the passage also talks about how some cultures may classify a story as a myth and others as a folktale.

The statement, from choice B, Traditional stories can be categorized in different ways by different people, is a more general statement that describes the passage.

14. B
Choice B is the best choice, categories that group traditional stories according to certain characteristics.

Choices A and C are false and can be eliminated right away. Choice D is designed to confuse. Choice D may be true, but it is not mentioned in the passage.

15. D
The best answer is D, traditional stories themselves are a part of the larger category of folklore, which may also include costumes, gestures, and music.

All the other choices are false. Traditional stories are part of the larger category of Folklore, which includes other things, not the other way around.

16. A
There is a distinct difference between a myth and a legend, although both are folktales.

17. A
Victoria is about 5 miles from Burnaby.

18. B
The Village Hall is about 5 miles from Victoria.

19. C
To be infamous means to be remembered for an evil or terrible action. Therefore, the word infamy means to remember a bad or terrible thing.

Choice A is incorrect because being famous is not the same as being infamous. Choice D is incorrect because Pearl Harbor was not forgotten.

20. C
Each other answer set contains the name of at least one country who was not part of the AXIS powers.

21. D
The answer is stated directly in the passage.

Choice A is in correct because there was no indication that Japan would attack San Diego. Choice B is incorrect because the attack on Pearl Harbor was a surprise. Choice C is incorrect because Roosevelt was not planning to attack Japan.

22. C
The passage clearly states that Japan planned a surprise attack. They chose that early time to catch the U.S. military off guard. Choice A is incorrect because the military does not sleep late. Choice B is incorrect because there is no law against bombing countries. Choice D is incorrect because it makes no sense.

23. B
This question tests the reader's summarization skills. A is a very broad statement that may or may not be true, and seems to be in context, but has nothing to do with the pas-

sage. The author does mention that the statue was probably used on a temple dedicated to the Greek gods (D), but in no way discusses or argues for the gods' attitude toward or claim on these temples or its faucets. Nike does indeed lead the gods into a war (the Titan war), as choice C suggests, but this is not mentioned by the passage and students who know this may be drawn to this answer but have not done a close enough analysis of the text that is actually in the passage. Choice B is appropriately expository, and connects the titular emphasis to the idea that the Greek gods are very important to Greek culture.

24. C
This question tests the reader's summarization skills. The test for question choice C is pulled straight from the paragraph, but is not word-for-word, so it may seem too obvious to be the right answer. The passage does talk about Nike being the goddess of war, as A states, but the third paragraph only touches on it and it is an inference that soldiers destroyed the statue, when this question is asking specifically for what the third paragraph actually stated. Choice B is also straight from the text, with a minor but key change: the inclusion of the words "all" and "never" are too limiting and the passage does not suggest that these limits exist. If a reader selects choice D, they are also making an inference that is misguided for this type of question. The paragraph does state that the arms and head are "lost" but does not suggest who lost them.

25. A
This question tests the reader's ability to recognize function in writing. Choice B can be eliminated based on the purpose of the passage, which is expository and not persuasive. The author may or may not feel this way, but the passage does not show evidence of being argumentative for that purpose. Choices C and D are both details found in the text, but neither of them encompasses the entire message of the passage, which has an overall message of learning about culture from art and making guesses about how the two are related, as suggested by choice A.

26. D
This question tests the reader's ability to understand func-

tion within writing. Most of the possible selections are very general statements which may or may not be true. It probably is a student who is taking the test on which this question is featured (A), but the author makes no address to the test taker and is not talking to the audience in terms of the test. Likewise, it may also be true that students read more than adults (C), mandated by schools and grades, but the focus on the verb "read" in the first sentence is too narrow and misses the larger purpose of the passage; the same could be said for choice B. While all the statements could be true, choice D is the most germane, and infers the purpose of the passage without making assumptions that could be incorrect.

27. B
The time limit for radar detectors is 14 days. Since you made the purchase 15 days ago, you do not qualify for the guarantee.

28. B
Since you made the purchase 10 days ago, you are covered by the guarantee. Since it is an advertised price at a different store, ABC Electric will "beat" the price by 10% of the difference, which is,

500 – 400 = 100 – difference in price

100 X 10% = $10 – 10% of the difference

The advertised lower price is $400. ABC will beat this price by 10% so they will refund $100 + 10 = $110.

29. C
The purpose of this passage is to persuade.

30. D
This question tests the reader's summarization skills. The question is asking very generally about the message of the passage, and the title, "Ways Characters Communicate in Theater," is one indication of that. The other choices A, B, and C are all directly from the text, and therefore readers may be inclined to select one of them, but are too specific to encapsulate the entirety of the passage and its message.

31. B

The paragraph on soliloquies mentions "To be or not to be," and it is from the context of that paragraph that readers may understand that because "To be or not to be" is a soliloquy, Hamlet will be introspective, or thoughtful, while delivering it. It is true that actors deliver soliloquies alone, and may be "solitary" (A), but "thoughtful" (B) is more true to the overall idea of the paragraph. Readers may choose choice C because drama and theater can be used interchangeably and the passage mentions that soliloquies are unique to theater (and therefore drama), but this answer is not specific enough to the paragraph in question. Readers may pick up on the theme of life and death and Hamlet's true intentions and select that he is "hopeless" (D), but those themes are not discussed either by this paragraph or passage, as a close textual reading and analysis confirms.

32. C

This question tests the reader's grammatical skills. Choice B seems logical, but parenthesis are actually considered to be a stronger break in a sentence than commas are, and along this line of thinking, actually disrupt the sentence more. Choices A and D make comparisons between theater and film that are simply not made in the passage, and may or may not be true. This detail does clarify the statement that asides are most unique to theater by adding that it is not completely unique to theater, which may have been why the author didn't chose not to delete it and instead used parentheses to designate the detail's importance (C).

33. C

This question tests the reader's vocabulary and contextualization skills. A may or may not be true, but focuses on the wrong function of the word "give" and ignores the rest of the sentence, which is more relevant to what the passage is discussing. Choices B and D may also be selected if the reader depends too literally on the word "give," failing to grasp the more abstract function of the word that is the focus of choice C, which also properly acknowledges the entirety of the passage and its meaning.

34. A
We can infer that an important purpose of the circulatory system is that of fighting diseases.

35. B
Humans have a closed circulatory system.

36. C
In addition to blood, the heart and the blood vessels form the cardiovascular system.

37. B
The digestive system, along with the circulatory system, helps provide nutrients to keep the human heart pumping.

38. A
We can infer that blood is responsible for transporting oxygen to the cells.

39. A
Human blood cells suspended in plasma.

40. C
Calcium is not contained in blood plasma.

From the passage, "[Blood Plasma] contains dissolved proteins, glucose, mineral ions, hormones, carbon dioxide, platelets and the blood cells themselves."

41. A
The lungs exhale the carbon dioxide after venous blood has been carried from body tissues.

42. A
The main idea of this passage is that the human skeleton is an important and complicated system of the body.

We can infer the skeleton is important because it protects important organs like brain, lungs and heart. We know the skeleton is complicated because it consists of several parts, (ligaments, tendons, muscles and cartilage) and 206 bones.

This general statement best describes the passage. The other choices are details mentioned in the passage.

Section II - Vocabulary

1. A
Verbiage NOUN speech with too many words.

2. A
Attache NOUN an aide or assistant.

3. A
Wreak VERB to cause or inflict especially related to harm or injury.

4. B
Witless ADJECTIVE foolish, without understanding.

5. A
Xenophobia NOUN a strong fear of strangers.

6. C
Zenith NOUN highest point, highest state or peak.

7. C
Zephyr NOUN light wind or gentle breeze.

8. A
Truism NOUN self evident or clear obvious truth.

9. A
Ulterior ADJECTIVE beyond what is obvious or evident.

10. D
Vapid ADJECTIVE tasteless or bland.

11. B
Waif NOUN homeless child or stray.

12. B
Whine VERB Complaint or criticism.

13. C
Underling NOUN subordinate of lesser rank or authority.

14. A
Yearling NOUN a young animal that is between 1 and 2 years.

15. B
Verdure NOUN lush green vegetation.

16. B
Zealot NOUN a person who is very passionate and fanatic about his specific objectives or beliefs.

17. C
Vertigo NOUN dizziness.

18. B
Conspicuous ADJECTIVE obvious or easy to notice.

19. D
Benevolence NOUN disposition to do good.

20. A
Boisterous ADJECTIVE full of energy; exuberant; noisy.

21. B
Fondle VERB to touch or stroke.

22. A
Momentous ADJECTIVE outstanding in importance.

23. A
Antagonist NOUN an opponent or enemy.

24. B
Memento NOUN a keepsake; an object kept as a reminder of a place or event.

25. C
Insidious ADJECTIVE producing harm in a stealthy, often gradual, manner.

26. C
Itinerary NOUN a route or proposed route of a journey.

27. D
Illustrious ADJECTIVE dignified.

28. A
Trenchant ADJECTIVE sharp deep cutting or biting.

29. D
Osculate VERB to kiss or related to kissing.

30. A
Mutation NOUN change or alteration.

31. B
Lithe ADJECTIVE flexible or plaint.

32. B
Resent VERB to express displeasure or indignation.

33. A
Chubby ADJECTIVE fat, plump and overweight.

34. A
Skittish ADJECTIVE fearful or timid.

35. A
Rambunctious ADJECTIVE harsh or rough sounding.

36. D
Causal ADJECTIVE indicating or expressing a cause.

37. B
Repressible ADJECTIVE able to be kept under restraint or control.

38. C
Amphibious ADJECTIVE living both on land and in water.

39. B
Galvanize VERB to imbue with life or animation.

40. A
Nuance NOUN a slight degree of difference in anything perceptible to the sense of the mind.

41. B
Obfuscate VERB to deliberately make more confusing in order to conceal the truth.

42. A
Plethora NOUN an excessive amount or number; an abundance.

43. D
Laceration NOUN an irregular open wound caused by a blunt impact to soft tissue.

44. B
Enshroud VERB to cover with (or as if with) a shroud.

45. A
Hasten VERB to move in a quick fashion.

46. C
Pliable ADJECTIVE soft, flexible, easily bent; formed, shaped or molded.

47. C
Carefree ADJECTIVE indifferent, careless, showing a lack of concern.

48. A
Rescind VERB to repeal, annul, or declare void; to take (something such as a rule or contract) out of effect.

49. B
Headstrong ADJECTIVE determined to do as one pleases, and not as others want.

50. B
Oblique ADJECTIVE not straightforward; indirect; obscure; hence, disingenuous; underhand; perverse; sinister.

51. C
Temper VERB to moderate or control.

52. B
Cryptic ADJECTIVE mystified or of an obscure nature.

53. A
Curtail VERB to shorten or abridge the duration of something; to truncate.

54. B
Heed VERB to mind; to regard with care; to take notice of; to attend to; to observe.

55. D
Oblivious ADJECTIVE lacking awareness; unmindful.

56. B
Podium NOUN a platform on which to stand, as when conducting an orchestra or preaching at a pulpit.

57. B
Boorish ADJECTIVE behaving as a boor; rough in manners; rude; uncultured.

58. A
Heresy NOUN a controversial or unorthodox opinion held by a member of a group, as in politics, philosophy or science.

59. B
Respite NOUN a brief interval of rest or relief.

60. B
Regicide VERB to kill a king.

61. D
Salient ADJECTIVE worthy of note or relevant.

62. B
Sedentary ADJECTIVE not moving or sitting in one place.

63. B
Sedulous ADJECTIVE dedicated and diligent.

64. A
Tincture NOUN alcoholic drink with plant extract used for medicine.

65. B
Truism NOUN self-evident or clear obvious truth.

66. B
Mutation NOUN change or alteration.

67. B
Alchemy NOUN medieval chemical philosophy aimed at trying to change metal into gold.

68. A
Benchmark NOUN a standard of measure.

69. B
Pudgy ADJECTIVE fat, plump and overweight.

70. A
Timorous ADJECTIVE fearful or timid.

71. D
Raucous ADJECTIVE harsh or rough sounding.

72. A
Abet VERB to aid, help.

73. A
Adorn VERB to decorate.

74. C
Allege VERB to say without proof.

75. B
Nomadic ADJECTIVE wandering.

76. D
Appease VERB to calm or satisfy.

77. A
Opulent ADJECTIVE ostentatiously rich and lavish.

78. A
Perfunctory ADJECTIVE with little interest or enthusiasm.

79. B
Flout VERB to disregard or disobey.

80. A
Indefatigable ADJECTIVE incapable of defeat.

How to Prepare for a Test

MOST STUDENTS HIDE THEIR HEADS AND PROCRASTINATE WHEN FACED WITH PREPARING FOR AN EXAMINATION, HOPING THAT SOMEHOW THEY WILL BE SPARED THE AGONY OF TAKING THAT TEST, ESPECIALLY IF IT IS A BIG ONE THAT THEIR FUTURES RELY ON. Avoiding the all-important test is what many students do best and unfortunately, they suffer the consequences because of their lack of preparation.

Test preparation requires strategy. It also requires a dedication to getting the job done. It is the perfect training ground for anyone planning a professional life. Besides having several reliable strategies, the wise student also has a clear goal in mind and knows how to accomplish it. These tried and true concepts have worked well and will make your test preparation easier.

The Study Approach.

Take responsibility for your own test preparation.

It is a common- but big - mistake to link your studying to someone else. Study partners are great, but only if they are reliable. It is your job to be prepared for the test, even if a study partner fails you. Do not allow others to distract you from your goals.

Prioritize the time available to study.

When do you learn best, early in the day or in the dark of night? Does your mind absorb and retain information most efficiently in small blocks of time, or do you require long stretches to get the most done? It is important to figure out the best blocks of time available to you when you can be the most productive. Try to consolidate activities to allow for longer periods of study time.

Find a quiet place where you will not be disturbed.

Do not try to squeeze in quality study time in any old location.

Find some place peaceful and with a minimum of distractions, such as the library, a park or even the laundry room. Good lighting is essential and you need to have comfortable seating and a desk surface large enough to hold your materials. It is probably not a great idea to study in your bedroom. You might be distracted by clothes on the floor, a book you have been planning to read, the telephone or something else. Besides, in the middle of studying, that bed will start to look very comfortable. Whatever you do, avoid using the bed as a place to study since you might fall asleep as a way of avoiding your work! That is the last thing that you should be doing during study time.

The exception is flashcards. By far the most productive study time is sitting down and studying and studying only. However, with flashcards you can carry them with you and make use of odd moments, like standing in line or waiting for the bus. This isn't as productive, but it really helps and is definately worth doing.

Determine what you need to study.

Gather together your books, your notes, your laptop and any other materials needed to focus on your study for this exam. Ensure you have everything you need so you don't waste time. Remember paper, pencils and erasers, sticky notes, bottled water and a snack. Keep your phone with you if you need it to find out essential information, but keep it turned off so others can't distract you.

Have a positive attitude.

It is essential that you approach your studies for the test with an attitude that says you will pass it. And pass it with flying colors! This is one of the most important keys to successful study strategy. Believing that you are capable actually helps you to become capable.

THE STRATEGY OF STUDYING
Make materials easy to review and access.

Consolidate materials to help keep your study area clutter free. If you have a laptop and a means of getting on line, you do not need a dictionary and thesaurus as well since those things are easily accessible via the internet. Go through written notes and consolidate those, as well. Have everything you need, but do not weigh yourself down with duplicates.

Review class notes.

Stay on top of class notes and assignments by reviewing them frequently. Re-writing notes can be a terrific study trick, as it helps lock in information. Pay special attention to any comments that have been made by the teacher. If a study guide has been made available as part of the class materials, use it! It will be a valuable tool to use for studying.

Estimate how much time you will need.

If you are concerned about the amount of time you have available it is a good idea to set up a schedule so that you do not get bogged down on one section and end without enough time left to study other things. Remember to schedule break time, and use that time for a little exercise or other stress reducing techniques.

Test yourself to determine your weaknesses.

Look online for additional assessment and evaluation tools available for a particular subject. Once you have determined areas of concern, you will be able to focus on studying the information they contain and just brush up on the other areas of the exam.

Mental Prep – How to Psych Yourself Up for a Test

Because tests contribute mightily to your final class grade or to whether you are accepted into a program, it is understandable that taking tests can create a great deal of anxiety for many students. Even students who know they have learned all the required material find their minds going blank as they stare at the words in the questions. One easy way to overcome that anxiety is to prepare mentally for the test. Mentally preparing for an exam is really not difficult. There are simple techniques that any student can learn to increase their chances of earning a great score on the day of the test.

Do not procrastinate.

Study the material for the test when it becomes available, and continue to review the material until the test day. By waiting until the last minute and trying to cram for the test the night before, you actually increase the amount of anxiety you feel. This leads to an increase in negative self-talk. Telling yourself "I can't learn this. I am going to fail" is a pretty sure indication that you are right. At best, your performance on the test will not be as strong if you have procrastinated instead of studying.

Positive self-talk.

Positive self-talk serves both to drown out negative self-talk and to increase your confidence in your abilities. Whenever you begin feeling overwhelmed or anxious about the test, remind yourself that you have studied enough, you know the material and that you will pass the test. Use only positive words. Both negative and positive self-talk are really just your fantasy, so why not choose to be a winner?

Do not compare yourself to anyone else.

Do not compare yourself to other students, or your performance to theirs. Instead, focus on your own strengths and weaknesses and prepare accordingly. Regardless of how others perform, your performance is the only one that matters to your grade. Comparing yourself to others increases your anxiety and your level of negative self-talk before the test.

Visualize.

Make a mental image of yourself taking the test. You know the answers and feel relaxed. Visualize doing well on the test and having no problems with the material. Visualizations can increase your confidence and decrease the anxiety you might otherwise feel before the test. Instead of thinking of this as a test, see it as an opportunity to demonstrate what you have learned!

Avoid negativity.

Worry is contagious and viral - once it gets started it builds on itself. Cut it off before it gets to be a problem. Even if you are relaxed and confident, being around anxious, worried classmates might cause you to start feeling anxious. Before the test, tune out the fears of classmates. Feeling anxious and worried before an exam is normal, and every student experiences those feelings at some point. However, you cannot allow these feelings to interfere with your ability to perform well. Practicing mental preparation techniques and remembering that the test is not the only measure of your academic performance will ease your anxiety and ensure that you perform at your best.

How to Take a Test

EVERYONE KNOWS THAT TAKING AN EXAM IS STRESSFUL, BUT IT DOES NOT HAVE TO BE THAT BAD! There are a few simple things that you can do to increase your score on any type of test. Take a look at these tips and consider how you can incorporate them into your study time.

Reading the Instructions

This is the most basic point, but one that, surprisingly, many students ignore and it can cost them big time! Since reading the instructions is one of the most common, and 100% preventable mistakes, we have a whole section just on reading instructions.

Pay close attention to the sample questions. Almost all standardized tests offer sample questions, paired with their correct solutions. Go through these to make sure that you understand what they mean and how they arrived at the correct answer. Do not be afraid to ask the test supervisor for help with a sample that confuses you, or instructions that you are unsure of.

Tips for Reading the Question

We could write pages and pages of tips just on reading the test questions. Here are the ones that will help you the most.

- **Think first.** Before you look at the answer, read and think about the question. It is best to try to come up with the correct answer before you look at the options given. This way, when the test-writer tries to trick you with a close answer, you will not fall for it.

- **Make it true or false.** If a question confuses you, then look at each answer option and think of it as a "true" "false" question. Select the one that seems most likely to be "true."

- **Mark the Question.** For some reason, a lot of test-takers are afraid to mark up their test booklet. Unless you are specifically told not to mark in the booklet, you should feel free to use it to your advantage. More on this below.

- **Circle Key Words.** As you are reading the question, underline or circle key words. This helps you to focus on the most critical information needed to solve the problem. For example, if the question said, "Which of these is not a synonym for huge?" You might circle "not," "synonym" and "huge." That clears away the clutter and lets you focus on what is important. More on this below.

- **Always underline these words:** all, none, always, never, most, best, true, false and except.

- **Cross out irrelevant choices.** If you find yourself confused by lengthy questions, cross out anything that you think is irrelevant, obviously wrong, or information that you think is offered to distract you.

- **Do not try to read between the lines.** Usually, questions are written to be straightforward, with no deep, underlying meaning. The simple answer really is often the correct answer. Do not over-analyze!

How to Take a Test - The Basics

Some tests are designed to assess your ability to quickly grab the necessary information; this type of exam makes speed a priority. Others are more concerned with your depth of knowledge, and how accurate it is. When you receive a test, look it over to determine whether the test is for speed or accuracy. If the test is for speed, like many standardized tests, your strategy is clear; answer as many questions as quickly as possible.

Watch out, though! There are a few tests that are designed to determine how fully and accurately you can answer the questions. Guessing on this type of test is a big mistake, because the teacher expects any student with an average grade to be able to complete the test in the time given. Racing through the test and making guesses that prove to be incorrect will cost you big time!

Every little bit helps.

If you are permitted calculators, or other materials, make sure you bring them, even if you do not think you will need them. Use everything at your disposal to increase your score.

Make time your friend.

Budget your time from the moment your pencil hits the page until you are finished with the exam, and stick to it! Virtually all standardized tests have a time limit for each section. The amount of time you are permitted for each portion of the test will almost certainly be included in the instructions or printed at the top of the page. If for some reason it is not immediately visible, rather than wasting your time hunting for it you can use the points or percentage of the score as a proxy to make an educated guess regarding the time limit.

Use the allotted time for each section and then move onto the next section whether you have completed the first section or not. Stick with the instructions and you will be able to answer most of the questions in each section.

With speed tests you may not be able to complete the entire test. Rest assured that you are not really expected to! The goal of this type of examination is to determine how quickly you can reach into your brain and access a particular piece of information, which is one way of determining how well you know it. If you know a test you are taking is a speed test, you will know the strategies to use for the best results.

Easy does it.

One smart way to tackle a test is to locate the easy questions and answer those first. This is a time-tested strategy that never fails, because it saves you a lot of unnecessary fretting. First, read the question and decide if you can answer it in less than a minute. If so, complete the question and go to the next one. If not, skip it for now and continue to the next question. By the time you have completed the first pass through this section of the exam, you will have answered a good number of questions. Not only does it boost your confidence, relieve anxiety and kick your memory up a notch, you will know exactly how many questions remain and can allot the rest of your time accordingly. Think of doing the easy questions first as a warm-up!

If you run out of time before you manage to tackle all the difficult questions, do not let it throw you. All that means is you have used your time in the most efficient way possible by answering as many questions correctly as you could. Missing a few points by not answering a question whose answer you do not know just means you spent that time answering one whose answer you did.

A word to the wise: Skipping questions for which you are drawing a complete blank is one thing, but we are not suggesting you skip every question you come across that you are not 100 % certain of. A good rule of thumb is to try to answer at least eight of every 10 questions the first time through.

Do not watch your watch.

At best, taking an important exam is an uncomfortable situation. If you are like most people, you might be tempted to subconsciously distract yourself from the task at hand. One of the most common ways to do so is by becoming obsessed with your watch or the wall clock. Do not watch your watch! Take it off and place it on the top corner of your desk, far enough away that you will not be tempted to look at it every two minutes. Better still, turn the watch face away from you. That way, every time you try to sneak a peek, you will be reminded to refocus your attention to the task at hand. Give yourself permission to check your watch or the wall clock after you complete each section. If you know yourself to be a bit of a slow-poke in other aspects of life, you can check your watch a bit more often. Even so, focus on answering the questions, not on how many minutes have elapsed since you last looked at it.

Divide and conquer.

What should you do when you come across a question that is so complicated you may not even be certain what is being asked? As we have suggested, the first time through the section you are best off skipping the question. However, at some point, you will need to return to it and get it under control. The best way to handle questions that leave you feeling so anxious you can hardly think is by breaking them into manageable pieces. Solving smaller bits is always easier. For complicated questions, divide them into bite-sized pieces and solve these smaller sets separately. Once you understand what the reduced sections are really saying, it will be much easier to put them together and get a handle on the bigger question.

Reason your way through the toughest questions.

If you find that a question is so dense you can't figure out how to break it into smaller pieces, there are a few strategies that might help. First, read the question again and look for hints. Can you re-word the question in one or more different ways? This may give you clues. Look for words that can function as either verbs or nouns, and try to figure out from the sentence structure which it is here. Remember that many nouns in English have several different meanings. While some of those meanings might be related, sometimes they are completely distinct. If reading the sentence one way does not make sense, consider a different definition or meaning for a key word.

The truth is, it is not always necessary to understand a question to arrive at a correct answer! A trick that successful students understand is using Strategy 5, Elimination. Frequently, at least one answer is clearly wrong and can be crossed off the list of possible correct answers. Next, look at the remaining answers and eliminate any that are only partly true. You may still have to flat-out guess from time to time, but using the process of elimination will help you make your way to the correct answer more often than not - even when you don't know what the question means!

Do not leave early.

Use all the time allotted to you, even if you can't wait to get out of the testing room. Instead, once you have finished, spend the remaining time reviewing your answers. Go back to those questions that were most difficult for you and review your response. Another good way to use this time is to return to multiple-choice questions in which you filled in a bubble. Do a spot check, reviewing every fifth or sixth question to make sure your answer coincides with the bubble you filled in. This is a great way to catch yourself if you made a mistake, skipped a bubble and therefore put all your answers in the wrong bubbles!

Become a super sleuth and look for careless errors. Look for questions that have double negatives or other odd phrasing; they might be an attempt to throw you off. Careless errors on your part might be the result of skimming a question and missing a key word. Words such as "always," "never," "sometimes," "rarely" and the like can give a strong indication of the answer the question is really seeking. Don't throw away points by being careless!

Just as you budgeted time at the beginning of the test to allow for easy and more difficult questions, be sure to budget sufficient time to review your answers. On essay questions and math questions where you are required to show your work, check your writing to make sure it is legible.

Math questions can be especially tricky. The best way to double check math questions is by figuring the answer using a different method, if possible.

Here is another terrific tip. It is likely that no matter how hard you try, you will have a handful of questions you just are not sure of. Keep them in mind as you read through the rest of the test. If you can't answer a question, looking back over the test to find a different question that addresses the same topic might give you clues.

We know that taking the test has been stressful and you can hardly wait to escape. Just keep in mind that leaving before you double-check as much as possible can be a quick trip to disaster. Taking a few extra minutes can make the difference between getting a bad grade and a great one. Besides, there will be lots of time to relax and celebrate after the test is turned in.

In the Test Room – What you MUST do!

If you are like the rest of the world, there is almost nothing you would rather avoid than taking a test. Unfortunately, that is not an option if you want to pass. Rather than suffer, consider a few attitude adjustments that might turn the experience from a horrible one to...well, an interesting one! Take a look at these tips. Simply changing how you perceive the experience can change the experience itself.

Get in the mood.

After weeks of studying, the big day has finally arrived. The worst thing you can do to yourself is arrive at the test site feeling frustrated, worried, and anxious. Keep a check on your emotional state. If your emotions are shaky before a test it can determine how well you do on the test. It is extremely important that you pump yourself up, believe in yourself, and use that confidence to get in the mood!

Don't fight reality.

Oftentimes, students resent tests, and with good reason. After all, many people do not test well, and they know the grade they end with does not accurately reflect their true knowledge. It is easy to feel resentful because tests classify students and create categories that just don't seem fair. Face it: Students who are great at rote memorization and not that good at actually analyzing material often score higher than those who might be more creative thinkers and balk at simply memorizing cold, hard facts. It may not be fair, but there it is anyway. Conformity is an asset on tests, and creativity is often a liability. There is no point in wasting time or energy being upset about this reality. Your first step is to accept the reality and get used to it. You will get higher marks when you realize tests do count and that you must give them your best effort. Think about your future and the career that is easier to achieve if you have consistently earned high grades. Avoid negative energy and focus on anything that lifts your enthusiasm and increases your motivation.

Get there early enough to relax.

If you are wound up, tense, scared, anxious, or feeling rushed, it will cost you. Get to the exam room early and relax before you go in. This way, when the exam starts, you are comfortable and ready to apply yourself. Of course, you do not want to arrive so early that you are the only one there. That will not help you relax; it will only give you too much time to sit there, worry and get wound up all over again.

If you can, visit the room where you will be taking your exam a few days ahead of time. Having a visual image of the room can be surprisingly calming, because it takes away one of the big 'unknowns,' Not only that, but once you have visited, you know how to get there and will not be worried about getting lost. Furthermore, driving to the test site once lets you know how much time you need to allow for the trip. That means three potential stressors have been eliminated all at once.

Get it down on paper.

One of the advantages of arriving early is that it allows you time to recreate notes. If you spend a lot of time worrying about whether you will be able to remember information like names, dates, places, and mathematical formulas, there is a solution for that. Unless the exam you are taking allows you to use your books and notes, (and very few do) you will have to rely on memory. Arriving early gives to time to tap into your memory and jot down key pieces of information you know will be asked. Just make certain you are allowed to make notes once you are in the testing site; not all locations will permit it. Once you get your test, on a small piece of paper write down everything you are afraid you will forget. It will take a minute or two but by dumping your worries onto the page you have effectively eliminated a certain amount of anxiety and driven off the panic you feel.

Get comfortable in your chair.

Here is a clever technique that releases physical stress and helps you get comfortable, even relaxed in your body. You will tense and hold each of your muscles for just a few seconds. The trick is, you must tense them hard for the technique to work. You might want to practice this technique a few times at home; you do not want an unfamiliar technique to add to your stress just before a test, after all! Once you are at the test site, this exercise can always be done in the rest room or another quiet location.

Start with the muscles in your face then work down your body. Tense, squeeze and hold the muscles for a moment or two. Notice the feel of every muscle as you go down your body. Scowl to tense your forehead, pull in your chin to tense your neck. Squeeze your shoulders down to tense your back. Pull in your stomach all the way back to your ribs, make your lower back tight then stretch your fingers. Tense your leg muscles and calves then stretch your feet and your toes. You should be as stiff as a board throughout your entire body.

Now relax your muscles in reverse starting with your toes. Notice how all the muscles feel as you relax them one by one. Once you have released a muscle or set of muscles, allow them to remain relaxed as you proceed up your body. Focus on how you are feeling as all the tension leaves. Start breathing deeply when you get to your chest muscles. By the time you have found your chair, you will be so relaxed it will feel like bliss!

Fight distraction.

A lucky few are able to focus deeply when taking an important examination, but most people are easily distracted, probably because they would rather be anyplace else! There are a number of things you can do to protect yourself from distraction.

Stay away from windows. If you select a seat near a window you may end gazing out at the landscape instead of paying attention to the work at hand. Furthermore, any sign of human activity, from a single individual walking by to a couple having an argument or exchanging a kiss will draw your attention away from your important work. What goes on outside should not be allowed to distract you.

Choose a seat away from the aisle so you do not become distracted by people who leave early. People who leave the exam room early are often the ones who fail. Do not compare your time to theirs.

Of course, you love your friends; that's why they are your friends! In the test room, however, they should become complete strangers inside your mind. Forget they are there. The first step is to physically distance yourself from friends or classmates. That way, you will not be tempted to glance at them to see how they are doing, and there will be no chance of eye contact that could either distract you or even lead to an accusation of cheating. Furthermore, if they are feeling stressed because they did not spend the focused time studying that you did, their anxiety is less likely to permeate your hard-earned calm.

Of course, you will want to choose a seat where there is sufficient light. Nothing is worse than trying to take an important examination under flickering lights or dim bulbs.

Ask the instructor or exam proctor to close the door if there is a lot of noise outside. If the instructor or proctor is unable to do so, block out the noise as best you can. Do not let anything disturb you.

Make sure you have enough pencils, pens and whatever else you will need. Many entrance exams do not permit you to bring personal items such as candy bars into the testing room. If this is the case with the exam you are sitting for, be sure to eat a nutritionally balanced breakfast. Eat protein, complex carbohydrates and a little fat to keep you feeling full and to supercharge your energy. Nothing is worse than a sudden drop in blood sugar during an exam.

Do not allow yourself to become distracted by being too cold or hot. Regardless of the weather outside, carry a sweater, scarf or jacket if the air conditioning at the test site is set too high, or the heat set too low. By the same token, dress in layers so that you are prepared for a range of temperatures.

Bring a watch so that you can keep track of time management. The danger here is many students become obsessed with how many minutes have passed since the last question. Instead of wearing the watch, remove it and place it in the far upper corner of the desk with the face turned away. That way, you cannot become distracted by repeatedly glancing at the time, but it is available if you need to know it.

Drinking a gallon of coffee or gulping a few energy drinks might seem like a great idea, but it is, in fact, a very bad one. Caffeine, pep pills or other artificial sources of energy are more likely to leave you feeling rushed and ragged. Your brain might be clicking along, all right, but chances are good it is not clicking along on the right track! Furthermore, drinking lots of coffee or energy drinks will mean frequent trips to the rest room. This will cut into the time you should be spending answering questions and is a distraction in itself, since each time you need to leave the room you lose focus. Pep pills will only make it harder for you to think straight when solving complicated problems on the exam.

At the same time, if anxiety is your problem try to find ways around using tranquilizers during test-taking time. Even medically prescribed anti-anxiety medication can make you less alert and even decrease your motivation. Being motivated is what you need to get you through an exam. If your anxiety is so bad that it threatens to interfere with your ability to take an exam, speak to your doctor and ask for documentation. Many testing sites will allow non-distracting test rooms, extended testing time and other accommodations since a doctor's note that explains the situation is made available.

Keep Breathing.

It might not make a lot of sense, but when people become anxious, tense, or scared, their breathing becomes shallow and, sometimes, they stop breathing all together! Pay attention to your emotions, and when you are feeling worried, focus on your breathing. Take a moment to remind yourself to breathe deeply and regularly. Drawing in steady, deep breaths energizes the body. When you continue to breathe deeply you will notice you exhale all the tension.

It is a smart idea to rehearse breathing at home. With continued practice of this relaxation technique, you will begin to know the muscles that tense up under pressure. Call these your "signal muscles." These are the ones that will speak to you first, begging you to relax. Take the time to listen to those muscles and do as they ask. With just a little breathing practice, you will get into the habit of checking yourself regularly and when you realize you are tense, relaxation will become second nature.

AVOID ANXIETY BEFORE A TEST

Manage your time effectively.

This is a key to your success! You need blocks of uninterrupted time to study all the pertinent material. Creating and maintaining a schedule will help keep you on track, and will remind family members and friends that you are not available. Under no circumstances should you change your blocks of study time to accommodate someone else, or cancel a study session to do something more fun. Do not interfere with your study time for any reason!

Relax.

Use whatever works best for you to relieve stress. Some folks like a good, calming stretch with yoga, others find expressing themselves through journaling to be useful. Some hit the floor for a series of crunches or planks, and still others take a slow stroll around the garden. Integrate a little relaxation time into your schedule, and treat that time, too, as sacred.

Eat healthy.

Instead of reaching for the chips and chocolate, fresh fruits and vegetables are not only yummy but offer nutritional benefits that help to relieve stress. Some foods accelerate stress instead of reducing it and should be avoided. Foods that add to higher anxiety include artificial sweeteners, candy and other sugary foods, carbonated sodas, chips, chocolate, eggs, fried foods, junk foods, processed foods, red meat, and other foods containing preservatives or heavy spices. Instead, eat a bowl of berries and some yogurt!

Get plenty of ZZZZZZZs.

Do not cram or try to do an all-nighter. If you created a study schedule at the beginning, and if you have stuck with that schedule, have confidence! Staying up too late trying to cram in last-minute bits of information is going to leave you exhausted the next day. Besides, whatever new information you cram in will only displace all the important ideas you've spent weeks learning. Remember: You need to be alert and fully functional the day of the exam

Eat a healthy meal before the exam.

Whatever you do - do not go into the test room hungry! Eat a meal that is rich in protein and complex carbohydrates before the test. Avoid sugary foods; they will pump you up initially, but you might crash hard part way through the exam. While you do not want to consume a lot of unhealthy fat, you do need a little of the healthy stuff such as flaxseed or olive oil on a salad. Avoid fried foods; they tend to make you sleepy.

Have confidence in yourself!

Everyone experiences some anxiety when taking a test, but exhibiting a positive attitude banishes anxiety and fills you with the knowledge you really do know what you need to know. This is your opportunity to show how well prepared you are. Go for it!

Be sure to take everything you need.

Depending on the exam, you may be allowed to have a pen or pencil, calculator, dictionary or scratch paper with you. Have these gathered together along with your entrance paperwork and identification so that you are sure you have everything that is needed.

Do not chitchat with friends.

Let your friends know ahead of time that it is not anything personal, but you are going to ignore them in the test room! You need to find a seat away from doors and windows, one that has good lighting, and get comfortable. If other students are worried their anxiety could be detrimental to you; of course, you do not have to tell your friends that. If you are afraid they will be offended, tell them you are protecting them from your anxiety!

Common Test-Taking Mistakes

Taking a test is not much fun at best. When you take a test and make a stupid mistake that negatively affects your grade, it is natural to be very upset, especially when it is something that could have been easily avoided. So what are some of the common mistakes that are made on tests?

Do not fail to put your name on the test.

How could you possibly forget to put your name on a test? You would be amazed at how often that happens. Very often, tests without names are thrown out immediately, resulting in a failing grade.

Not following directions.

Directions are carefully worded. If you skim directions, it is very easy to miss key words or misinterpret what is being said. Nothing is worse than failing an examination simply because you could not be bothered with reading the instructions!

Marking the wrong multiple-choice answer.

It is important to work at a steady pace, but that does not mean bolting through the questions. Be sure the answer you are marking is the one you mean to. If the bubble you need to fill in or the answer you need to circle is 'C', do not allow yourself to get distracted and select 'B' instead.

Answering a question twice.

Some multiple-choice test questions have two very similar answers. If you are in too much of a hurry, you might select them both. Remember that only one answer is correct, so if you choose more than one, you have automatically failed that question.

Mishandling a difficult question.

We recommend skipping difficult questions and returning to them later, but beware! First, be certain that you do return to the question. Circling the entire passage or placing a large question mark beside it will help you spot it when you are reviewing your test. Secondly, if you are not careful to actually skip the question, you can mess yourself up badly. Imagine that a question is too difficult and you decide to save it for later. You read the next question, which you know the answer to, and you fill in that answer. You continue to the end of the test then return to the difficult question only to discover you didn't actually skip it! Instead, you inserted the answer to the following question in the spot reserved for the harder one, thus throwing off the remainder of your test!

Incorrectly Transferring an answer from scratch paper.

This can happen easily if you are trying to hurry! Double check any answer you have figured out on scratch paper, and make sure what you have written on the test itself is an exact match!

Don't ignore the clock, and don't marry it, either.

In a timed examination many students lose track of the time and end without sufficient time to complete the test. Remember to pace yourself! At the same time, though, do not allow yourself to become obsessed with how much time has elapsed, either.

Thinking too much.

Oftentimes, your first thought is your best thought. If you worry yourself into insecurity, your self-doubts can trick you into choosing an incorrect answer when your first impulse was the right one!

Be prepared.

Running out of ink and not having an extra pen or pencil is not an excuse for failing an exam! Have everything you need, and have extras. Bring tissue, an extra eraser, several sharpened pencils, batteries for electronic devices, and anything else you might need.

Do not fail to put your name on the test.

How could you possibly forget to put your name on a test? You would be amazed at how often that happens. Very often, tests without names are thrown out immediately, resulting in a failing grade.

Not following directions.

Directions are carefully worded. If you skim directions, it is very easy to miss key words or misinterpret what is being said. Nothing is worse than failing an examination simply because you could not be bothered with reading the instructions!

Marking the wrong multiple-choice answer.

It is important to work at a steady pace, but that does not mean bolting through the questions. Be sure the answer you are marking is the one you mean to. If the bubble you need to fill in or the answer you need to circle is 'C', do not allow yourself to get distracted and select 'B' instead.

Answering a question twice.

Some multiple-choice test questions have two very similar answers. If you are in too much of a hurry, you might select them both. Remember that only one answer is correct, so if you choose more than one, you have automatically failed that question.

Mishandling a difficult question.

We recommend skipping difficult questions and returning to them later, but beware! First, be certain that you do return to the question. Circling the entire passage or placing a large question mark beside it will help you spot it when you are reviewing your test. Secondly, if you are not careful to actually skip the question, you can mess yourself up badly. Imagine that a question is too difficult and you decide to save it for later. You read the next question, which you know the answer to, and you fill in that answer. You continue to the end of the test then return to the difficult question only to discover you didn't actually skip it! Instead, you inserted the answer to the following question in the spot reserved for the harder one, thus throwing off the remainder of your test!

Incorrectly Transferring an answer from scratch paper.

This can happen easily if you are trying to hurry! Double check any answer you have figured out on scratch paper, and make sure what you have written on the test itself is an exact match!

Don't ignore the clock, and don't marry it, either.

In a timed examination many students lose track of the time and end without sufficient time to complete the test. Remember to pace yourself! At the same time, though, do not allow yourself to become obsessed with how much time has elapsed, either.

Thinking too much.

Oftentimes, your first thought is your best thought. If you worry yourself into insecurity, your self-doubts can trick you into choosing an incorrect answer when your first impulse was the right one!

Be prepared.

Running out of ink and not having an extra pen or pencil is not an excuse for failing an exam! Have everything you need, and have extras. Bring tissue, an extra eraser, several sharpened pencils, batteries for electronic devices, and anything else you might need.

Be sure to take everything you need.

Depending on the exam, you may be allowed to have a pen or pencil, calculator, dictionary or scratch paper with you. Have these gathered together along with your entrance paperwork and identification so that you are sure you have everything that is needed.

Do not chitchat with friends.

Let your friends know ahead of time that it is not anything personal, but you are going to ignore them in the test room! You need to find a seat away from doors and windows, one that has good lighting, and get comfortable. If other students are worried their anxiety could be detrimental to you; of course, you do not have to tell your friends that. If you are afraid they will be offended, tell them you are protecting them from your anxiety!

Conclusion

CONGRATULATIONS! You have made it this far because you have applied yourself diligently to practicing for the exam and no doubt improved your potential score considerably! Getting into a good school is a huge step in a journey that might be challenging at times but will be many times more rewarding and fulfilling. That is why being prepared is so important.

Study then Practice and then Succeed!

Good Luck!

Thanks!

If you enjoyed this book and would like to order additional copies for yourself or for friends, please check with your local bookstore, favorite online bookseller or visit www.test-preparation.ca and place your order directly with the publisher.

Feedback to the author may be sent by email to feedback@test-preparation.ca

Endnotes

Text where noted below is used under the Creative Commons Attribution-ShareAlike 3.0 License

http://en.wikipedia.org/wiki/Wikipedia:Text_of_Creative_Commons_Attribution-ShareAlike_3.0_Unported_License

[1] The Immune System. In *Wikipedia*. Retrieved Feb 14, 2009, from http://en.wikipedia.org/wiki/Immune_system.
[2] White Blood Cell. In *Wikipedia*. Retrieved Feb 14, 2009, from http://en.wikipedia.org/wiki/White_blood_cell.
[3] Thunderstorm. In *Wikipedia*. Retrieved Feb 14, 2009, from
http://en.wikipedia.org/wiki/Thunderstorm/
[4] Wiktionary. Retrieved Feb 14, 2009, from http://http://en.wiktionary.org/wiki/.
[4] Spider. In *Wikipedia*. Retrieved Feb 14, 2009, from http://en.wikipedia.org/wiki/Spider.
[5] Infectious Disease. In *Wikipedia*. Retrieved Feb 14, 2009, from
http://en.wikipedia.org/wiki/Infectious_disease.
[6] Virus. In *Wikipedia*. Retrieved Feb 14, 2009, from http://en.wikipedia.org/wiki/Virus.
[7] Outline of Meteorology. In *Wikipedia*. Retrieved Feb 14, 2009, from
http://en.wikipedia.org/wiki/Outline_of_meteorology.
[8] Butterfly. In *Wikipedia*. Retrieved Feb 14, 2009, from http://http://en.wikipedia.org/wiki/Butterfly.
[9] United States Navy SEALs. In *Wikipedia*. Retrieved Feb 14, 2009, from
http://en.wikipedia.org/wiki/United_States_Navy_SEALs.
[10] Respiratory System. In *Wikipedia*. Retrieved Feb 14, 2009, from
http://en.wikipedia.org/wiki/Respiratory_system.
[11] Mythology. In *Wikipedia*. Retrieved Feb 14, 2009, from http://en.wikipedia.org/wiki/Mythology.
[12] Insects. In *Wikipedia*. Retrieved Feb 14, 2009, from

http://en.wikipedia.org/wiki/Insect.

[13] Tree. In *Wikipedia*. Retrieved Feb 14, 2009, from http://en.wikipedia.org/wiki/Tree.

[14] List of Greek and Latin Roots in English. In *Wikipedia*. Retrieved Feb 14, 2009, from http://en.wikipedia.org/wiki/List_of_Greek_and_Latin_roots_in_English.

[15] What is Free Range Chicken In *Answers.com*. Retrieved Feb 14, 2009, from http://wiki.answers.com/Q/What_is_free-range_chicken.

[16] Grizzly Bear. In *Wikipedia*. Retrieved Feb 14, 2009, from http://en.wikipedia.org/wiki/Grizzly_Bear.

[17] Grizzly Polar Bear Hybrid. In *Wikipedia*. Retrieved Feb 14, 2009, from http://en.wikipedia.org/wiki/Grizzly%E2%80%93polar_bear_hybrid.

[18] Peafowl. In *Wikipedia*. Retrieved Feb 14, 2009, from en.wikipedia.org/wiki/Peafowl.

[19] Smallpox. In *Wikipedia*. Retrieved Feb 14, 2009, from http://en.wikipedia.org/wiki/Smallpox.

[20] Lightning. In *Wikipedia*. Retrieved Feb 14, 2009, from http://en.wikipedia.org/wiki/Lightning.

[21] Venus. In *Wikipedia*. Retrieved Feb 14, 2009, from http://en.wikipedia.org/wiki/Venus.

[22] Weather. In *Wikipedia*. Retrieved Feb 14, 2009, from http://en.wikipedia.org/wiki/Weather.

www.ingramcontent.com/pod-product-compliance
Lightning Source LLC
Chambersburg PA
CBHW072157090426
42740CB00012B/2299